PARADOXUM MUNDI

WHERE ART AND SCIENCE BLUR INTO ONE

THEA D.D

Made with ♥ on the Notion Press Platform
www.notionpress.com

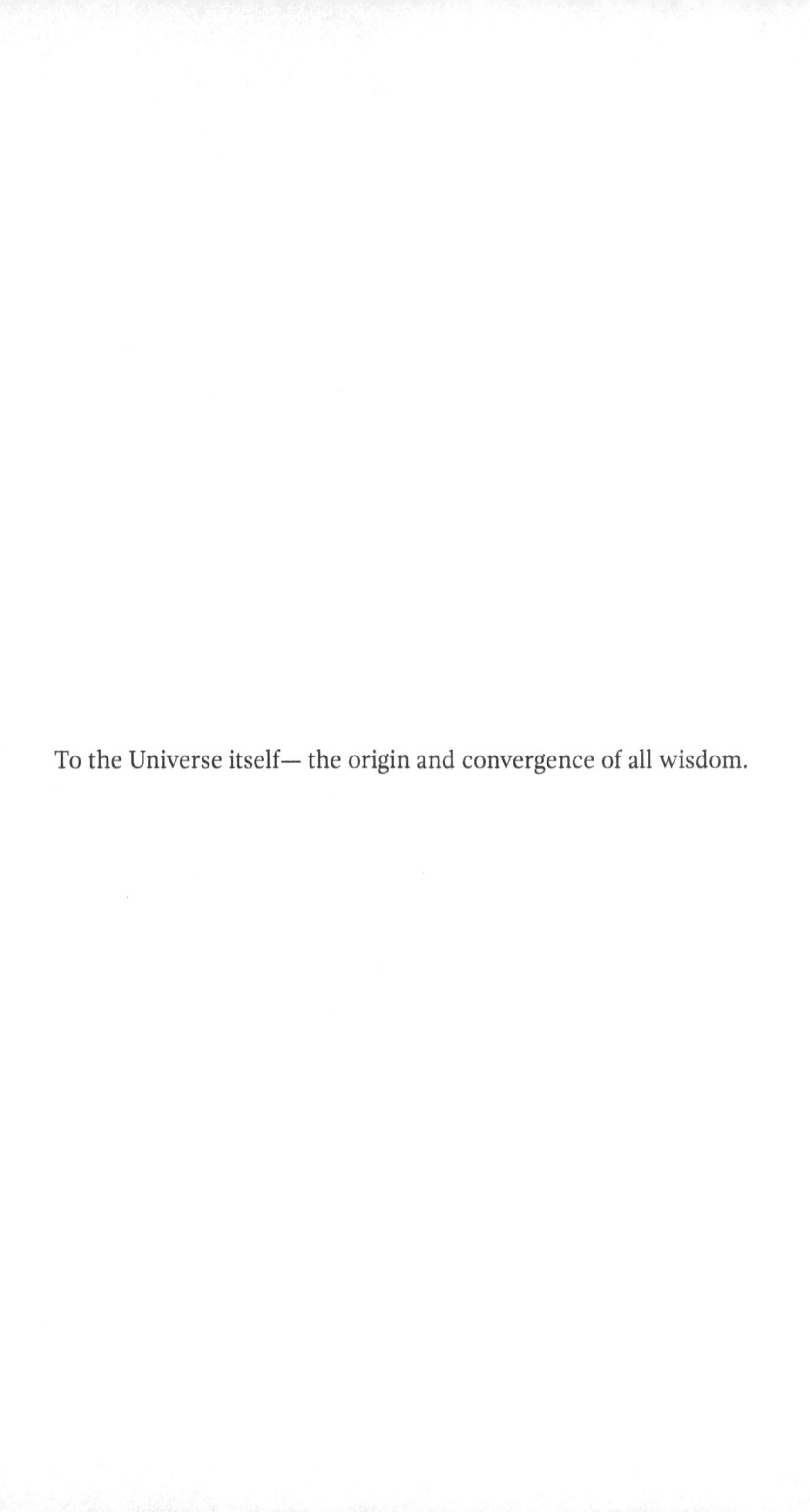

To the Universe itself— the origin and convergence of all wisdom.

Contents

Contents

Contents

Contents

Author (Theadra D.D)

Preface

"This book is not for those who sleep soundly in the comfort of the known world. It is for those who wake in the night, haunted by questions they cannot name. Proceed only if you are willing to see—truly see. Once you step forward, you may never return the same."

Acknowledgements

A letter to the seeker and gratitude .

Bonjour . I am not a mere girl writing this book. I am beyond this illusion of body and age, my wisdom stretching far beyond the limits of a number. I have lived more lives than this one, carried more questions than answers, and walked through both light and abyss.

I have experienced everything from a very young age. I have been a saint, and I have been a storm. I have been a girl with no modesty, sharp-edged and unyielding, and I have been one whose manners and behavior have been idealized,loved and respected. I have known fear that crippled me, and I have known fearlessness that burned like fire in my veins. I have been on the edge of death at seven. But then i was given a second life. A life of endless, unspoken mysteries, a life that was never ordinary. That is what shaped me into who I am today. I have been complete paradoxes woven into one. So, does wisdom come from within or from all that I have lived?I have manifested things that should not be possible. I have seen and felt what this world refuses to believe in. Supernatural? Perhaps. *No, this is not a story.* This is me. There is more to me than these words can hold, more than I will ever reveal. But this book, it is not about me. It is about you. Your journey.

Still, I must give thanks, to those who shaped this path before me.

To the books I have red , to the scientists who dared to rewrite the rules, to the ancient texts that left their secrets in plain sight for those willing to see. To the endless archives of knowledge, both hidden and open, that fueled my search.To the invention of internet .To my grandfather, who made me see through the veils . Who taught me to have faith in my mind, to question what is told, to see beyond what is given.To the mysterious man whose name I cannot reveal—who opened the doors of the universe and the soul before me. Who whispered secrets not meant for all ears. Who made me unsee the world as it was and reimagine it as it could be.To the TED Talks I have listened to, scribbling down notes in the dark of the night, piecing together wisdom from those who have seen further than most.And to myself. For refusing to settle, for walking paths no one handed to me, for standing alone when no one understood. For being foolish enough to seek the unknown, and wise enough to know that the search will never end.

Prologue

A personal note .

You've crossed the threshold. That was your choice, and now there's no return.What you hold in your hands is not just ink on paper. It is a key. A cipher. A test.This book will not teach you—it will unravel you.The answers are not given; they are hidden. Some pages whisper. Some scream. Some will wait for you to read between the lines.The veil of illusion will be unravelled.

If you have ever felt that the world was incomplete, if you have ever sensed the weight of something unspoken, then you already know.What if I told you that everything you were taught about the world was a half-truth at best, a deception at worst? That history is incomplete. That science is missing its other half. That art is more than beauty—it is the language of creation itself.

The greatest minds—Da Vinci, Tesla, Hypatia, Pythagoras understood this. They saw the hidden threads tying the universe together. And so did the ones before them, the ones who built impossible structures, left behind cryptic messages, and vanished into legend. If you have ever questioned why the pyramids echo the constellations, why Saturn hums in frequencies beyond our hearing, why certain paintings seem to speak, then you are already on the path.

And now, we walk it together.

But not everyone can make this till the end , the weight of knowledge and the unsolved mysteries can be heavy. ***And if you make it till the end then the truth ,perhaps something bigger awaits you .***

Foreword

Paradoxum Mundi doesn't just share ideas. It rewires how you think. It breaks down the walls between science, emotion, logic, and mystery and shows you the deeper patterns that control everything.

Most people live in loops that are repeating thoughts, habits, relationships. They think they're free, but they're not. This book exposes those loops. It teaches you to see the structure behind chaos. Once you see it, you can't unsee it.

That's why Paradoxum Mundi is dangerous.

It's for those who feel like there's more , more behind the patterns of life, love, power, time, death. People who want control over their mind, who are tired of being told how to think. If that's you, this book will feel like home.

It blends logic with emotion, science with soul. It speaks to the part of you that knows there's something deeper... but hasn't had the words for it , *until now.*

Read this if you want to think clearly in a noisy world.
Read this if you want to break free from what society trained you to be.
Read this if you want to remember who you really are.

This book won't make you comfortable. It will make you aware. And awareness is the first step to power.

CHAPTER ONE

SCIENTIA ET ARS

(The Silent Bond of Science & Art)

"The Unseen Equations of Beauty and Truth"

The Forbidden Truth

They will tell you that science and art are separate. That one is precise, sharp-edged, a world of formulas and cold logic. That the other is wild, untamed, born from emotion rather than reason. They lie.

They'll tell you science and art are separate. That one is cold, exact, and logical, while the other is emotional and free. But that's not true.

History proves it. The greatest minds never picked just one path. Pythagoras, the father of mathematics, saw numbers as music—patterns that made up the universe. Michelangelo didn't just paint; he studied the human body like a doctor. Every detail in the Sistine Chapel came from deep knowledge of muscles and bones. And Ada Lovelace, the world's first programmer, was also a poet. She didn't see numbers as dull. To her, they were full of creative power—like poetry that could build entire worlds.

Science and art aren't opposites. Together, they shape everything.

Why, then, are we asked to choose?

Perhaps because those who see beyond categories, who refuse to be confined to one way of thinking, are the ones who cannot be controlled. When an artist understands physics, they design cathedrals that stand for millennia. When a scientist thinks like a poet, they unlock the deepest layers of reality. That is dangerous. That is power. So they try to divide us. They tell the scientist that emotion has no place in their equations. They tell the artist that logic will kill their creativity. But the truth is far simpler, a mind that embraces both is unstoppable.

And so I ask you, when did they teach you to pick a side? When did they whisper that you could only be one thing?

Because i saw these paradoxes as one. Through my lenses Art and science has always been one or atleast connected . Its not only me that believes this but the most profound scientists , the ancient history and some of the most intriguing artifacts prove this. Nows lets shatter the illusion through this journey.

“The greatest scientists are artists as well.” — Albert Einstein

The Code Hidden in Beauty

There is a language older than words, more precise than numbers, yet effortlessly poetic. It is a language that has been whispered into the spirals of galaxies, the veins of leaves, the arches of forgotten cathedrals. You have seen it before, but perhaps you never realized it. Look at a seashell. Not just at its surface, but at its structure. The way it curls in perfect harmony, never rushed, never erratic. This is not randomness. This is mathematics, the Fibonacci sequence, nature's silent architect. The same sequence governs the petals of a rose, the branching of trees, the proportions of the human face. And yet, no poet would dare call a rose 'mathematical,' nor would a scientist think of a seashell as 'art.'

But what else could they be?

Stand before the Great Pyramid of Giza, and you will find that its dimensions align almost perfectly with the golden ratio—a proportion so mysteriously perfect that it has appeared in art, architecture, and even the spiral of our very DNA. Was this by chance? Or did the ancient minds who built it understand something we have forgotten?

Even music, one of the purest forms of human expression, is bound by invisible numbers. A symphony, no matter how hauntingly beautiful, follows precise mathematical patterns. The chords that stir your soul, the rhythm that sets your heartbeat in sync, are dictated by frequencies, ratios, and waveforms. *"Art is science in disguise. Science is art in structure."*

Yet, modern minds have been trained to ignore these connections.

A physicist studies light, calculating wavelengths, analyzing reflections, reducing brilliance to mere data. But an artist—an artist sees how light plays on silk, how it melts into shadow, how a single stroke of gold can make a canvas glow as if it holds the sun itself. Both are correct. Both understand light. But only together do they capture its true essence.

There was a time when we knew this. When alchemists were poets, when mathematicians sculpted wonders, when knowledge was not divided into 'useful' and 'beautiful.' That time is gone. But it does not have to be forgotten. If you have ever found beauty in logic, or reason in art, then you already hold the key.

The question is, will you use it?

The Mind That Sees Both

There is a certain kind of mind that history fears and yet cannot ignore. A mind that does not think in straight lines but in spirals, weaving between logic and imagination, precision and poetry. This mind is not common, nor is it welcome in a world that demands neat labels and clear divisions.

It belongs to those who see the patterns others miss.

I have always been drawn to this way of thinking, perhaps because I've never been able to settle for just one thing. The world tells you to choose. Be a scientist, be an artist, but never both. But why? When history is filled with people who saw the world through both lenses, who refused to be one-dimensional?

Take Nikola Tesla. To most, he was a scientist, a man of formulas and electric currents. But in truth, he was an artist of energy. He saw his inventions not as mere machines, but as symphonies of movement and light. He dreamed of harnessing the Earth's natural resonance, not with cold calculations alone, but with a vision so grand it bordered on the mystical.

Or consider Johannes Kepler. The father of planetary motion, his equations unlocked some of the profound knowledge of universe . But what few realize is that he was guided not just by mathematics, but by music. He believed the planets moved in harmonic ratios, composing an eternal, silent song—a theory known as the "Music of the Spheres." Numbers and melody, equations and rhythm—he saw no difference.And how many of us really know this ?

Even the great Marie Curie, a name synonymous with science, held a poetic obsession with light. She once wrote about how radium, the element she discovered, "shines with a faint blue light, as if it were alive." The way she spoke of her work, with awe rather than mere observation, reveals the truth—she was not just uncovering facts; she was chasing beauty in its purest form.

And so, the question lingers—why do we resist this way of thinking?

Perhaps because it demands too much. It is easier to be just one thing. To call oneself a scientist and dismiss the abstract, or to be an artist who rejects the rigid rules of logic. To embrace both is to live in constant tension, to be misunderstood, to belong everywhere and nowhere at once.

But those who dare to see the world through this lens—they are the ones who rewrite the rules. You are standing at the doorway of such a mind. The choice is yours—step through, or turn away.

But know this: once you see the world in both numbers and brushstrokes, you can never unsee it.

The Eyes That Notice

I have always been fascinated by the way some people walk through life blind to the details—oblivious to the way light bends through a raindrop or how the rhythm of footsteps on a marble floor mimics a heartbeat. They see only what is obvious, never questioning, never noticing. But then there are others—those who see the invisible, who can sense the architecture behind beauty, who realize that what looks effortless is often a masterpiece of hidden precision.

I think about the stained-glass windows of old cathedrals i have seen in movies, how the light filters through them at just the right angles, creating a celestial glow. To the untrained eye, it's simply breathtaking. But to someone who understands the science behind it, it's more than that—it's physics, it's geometry, it's the perfect interplay of wavelengths and glass density.

Or take a dancer on stage. To most, she is simply graceful, effortless in her movements. But behind that illusion of ease lies biomechanics, muscle memory, and an intuitive understanding of motion that even the greatest physicists would struggle to describe.

The truth is, the world rewards those who see deeply—who look beyond the surface and recognize the hidden design in everything.

Leonardo da Vinci did this. He wasn't just an artist; he was an anatomist, an engineer, an observer of both human expression and mechanical precision. His paintings weren't just beautiful—they were biologically accurate, mathematically balanced, designed with the kind of detail that only someone who understood both art and science could achieve.While reading his notebooks i came to know how skillful he was being a polymath.

I wonder—how many people pass by these things every day, never realizing the intelligence woven into them?

To notice is to hold power.

Because once you learn to see the structure behind beauty and the art behind logic, you can never be fooled by appearances again. You begin to see what others don't. You recognize patterns, connections, secrets hidden in plain sight.

And once you do, the world is no longer the same. It is richer. Deeper. Alive.

And dear readers this is the secret . Simple , but you can write many complex books explaining this SIMPLE SECRET.

The Caged Mind

There was a time when knowledge was seamless—when to be a thinker meant to be everything at once. The artist was a scientist, the mathematician was a poet, the philosopher was an architect of thought. There were no boundaries, no rigid compartments. Just curiosity and the hunger to understand.

But the world fears what it cannot control. And so, it built walls.

Modern academia thrives on division. Science is kept away from art, logic is stripped of beauty, and those who dare to blur the lines are quietly pushed aside. A physicist who speaks of emotion is romanticized, but never taken seriously. An artist who understands chemistry is labeled "unconventional" rather than brilliant. Schools do not teach us to think expansively—they teach us to specialize, to pick a side, to exist within predefined limits.

Because a mind that is whole—a mind that moves effortlessly between precision and passion—is a mind that is dangerous.

The Fallacy of Separation: A System by Design

Now the question is that if there was such a time then when did the division really happen ?

This artificial separation of disciplines did not happen by accident. It was a slow, calculated process shaped by industrialization, politics, and the desire for control. During the Enlightenment, polymaths like Isaac Newton and Gottfried Wilhelm Leibniz seamlessly blended mathematics, philosophy, and theology. But as society shifted towards mass education and the industrial age demanded specialized labor, a divide was enforced. Universities began structuring knowledge into distinct faculties, each with rigid boundaries.

By the 20th century, this compartmentalization was deeply ingrained. C.P. Snow's famous lecture The Two Cultures (1959) lamented how science and the humanities had become isolated from one another, creating an intellectual rift that limited progress. He argued that scholars of literature dismissed scientists as "mechanical" and scientists saw artists as "unserious." This divide, he warned, would cripple society's ability to address complex global challenges.

And yet, those who bridged the gap—like Richard Feynman, who found joy in both theoretical physics and painting—were seen as anomalies rather than the ideal. They were outliers, exceptions to the rule. But were they? Or was the rule itself a restriction designed to keep people from realizing the full capacity of their minds?

What They Fear: The Uncontrollable Thinker

The great minds of history were rarely obedient. They did not merely accept knowledge—they questioned it. They did not see subjects as isolated islands but as interconnected landscapes, where one insight could unlock a thousand doors.

Consider Leonardo da Vinci. He was not just a painter but an anatomist, an engineer, a visionary. His notebooks, filled with sketches of flying machines centuries before aviation,they proved that a limitless mind thrives beyond academic boundaries. He was not interested in "art" or "science" as separate entities—he was interested in truth.

Then there was Nikola Tesla, a man who saw electricity not just as a scientific force but as a means to revolutionize human existence. He dreamed of free energy, of an interconnected world. His ideas threatened those who profited from limitation. And so, he was discredited, cast aside, his innovations hidden away.

Even today, we see this fear manifest in subtle ways. Visionaries who challenge conventional thinking are labeled as “idealistic” or “impractical.” Those who attempt to merge disciplines are met with skepticism. The world does not like minds that roam freely—it prefers minds that comply.

The Books They Don’t Want You to Read

Knowledge is not just power. It is freedom. And those who wish to keep power tightly held understand this.

Certain books throughout history have challenged this artificial divide and, unsurprisingly, have been either ignored or subtly pushed out of mainstream education. Thomas Kuhn’s The Structure of Scientific Revolutions (1962) showed that science advances not by slowly adding facts but through sudden shifts in thinking. This challenges academia, which relies on the illusion of steady progress.

Then there is Gödel, Escher, Bach: An Eternal Golden Braid by Douglas Hofstadter—a book that defies categorization. It blends mathematics, music, and philosophy to reveal the deep interconnections of human thought. It is the kind of book that, if widely embraced, would shatter the way education is structured today.

Marshall McLuhan’s The Medium is the Message reveals that the way knowledge is delivered shapes what people see as important. The structure of information itself influences what we believe to be true. If society teaches people to think in separate categories, they may never question whether those divisions are real. And this is what we can truly relate .

Breaking the Cage: What Comes Next

The world is built to discourage minds that see too much. It rewards obedience and punishes the untamed. But history does not remember the obedient. It remembers the ones who refused to be confined. The ones who painted the human body while studying its inner mechanics. The ones who spoke of atoms while writing poetry. The ones who never asked, "Which side am I on?" but instead declared, "There are no sides. There is only knowing."

And so, the question is not whether you fit into the boxes the world has created.

The question is—will you destroy them, will you choose to have your own perspective, will you choose to see through the veil ?

CHAPTER TWO

CARNIS

(Echoes of the flesh)

"Deciphering Nature's Hidden Blueprint"

The Brain's Conspiracy

If you think that art belongs to feeling and science to reason. That the poet and the physicist walk separate roads. That biology is the study of life, but poetry is its expression. That a doctor and a painter cannot see the world through the same lens.

You are wrong . Look closer. The universe does not divide itself the way humans do.

Case Study I: The Music of Surgery

In the 1990s, a team of researchers at the University of Texas Medical Branch made an unusual discovery. Surgeons who played musical instruments had steadier hands than those who didn't. The precision required to play Bach's fugues or Paganini's caprices trained the nervous system to control micro-movements, making incisions smoother, stitches finer.

It was never just about the hands. The human brain processes movement the way it processes music—through rhythm, tempo, and spatial awareness. This is why elite neurosurgeons, like Dr. Charlie Teo, have compared their craft to composing a symphony. Each incision is a note, each stitch a measure, each operation an entire composition.

A contradiction? No. A convergence.

Case Study II: The Painter in the Lab

Barbara McClintock, the Nobel Prize-winning geneticist, saw DNA not as rigid code, but as a fluid, dynamic, living manuscript. She was the first to prove that genes could move—jumping from one chromosome to another like brushstrokes being rearranged on a canvas. Her colleagues, limited by the rigid mindset of the time, dismissed her findings for years.

But McClintock was not just a scientist; she was an artist. She spoke of genes as "music in motion", of DNA as an evolving tapestry rather than a machine. She was right. Today, her discovery of "jumping genes" (transposons) is fundamental to our understanding of genetic evolution. She did not think like a traditional scientist—she thought like a creator.

Case Study III: The Octopus That Paints With Light

The common cuttlefish does not see color the way we do. It lacks color receptors entirely. Yet, it can change its skin to match any shade in its surroundings—blues, purples, emerald greens—without ever perceiving them the way a human does.

How?

Inside its skin are chromatophores, pigment cells that expand and contract like a painter adjusting the pressure of a brushstroke. But hidden beneath those lie iridophores and leucophores—cells that manipulate light itself, bending wavelengths, reflecting hues that the creature has never seen. The cuttlefish does not copy color. It creates it. This is not just biology. This is art in motion—evolution sculpting its own masterpiece.

And are you aware of the fact that the structure of your lungs follows fractal mathematics—the same patterns seen in river deltas and tree branches. Your neurons communicate in waves like the ripples of a pond, obeying the laws of interference that govern both sound and light.

Everywhere you look, science is art. Art is science.The division was never real.If you wish to create—to truly create—you must unlearn the separation they taught you. You are not either a scientist or an artist. ***You are both***. You always have been. The world just convinced you otherwise.

The Language of the Universe

You were taught to read letters. But before humanity carved its first script into clay, the universe had already written its own. Its alphabet is the spiral of a galaxy, the rhythm of a heartbeat, the branching of neurons. Its language is not spoken but observed.

Case Study I: The Mathematician Who Heard Colors

The year was 1842. A young woman named Sophie Germain sat in the dim glow of candlelight, her hands tracing patterns over parchment. She had no formal training as women then were not allowed in mathematical circles,but she had something more valuable: an untrained mind that saw patterns where others saw rules. She discovered that vibrations in metal plates followed the same harmonic sequences found in music. She hypothesized that the structure of matter itself could be predicted using these harmonics and that *form was merely frozen sound.* She was dismissed, uncredited for years. Yet today, her work laid the foundation for acoustic engineering, quantum mechanics, and even the study of black holes. She did not see numbers. She saw music.

The universe speaks in frequencies—most people just don't listen.

Case Study II: The Tree That Calculates

Step into a dense rainforest, and you'll find fig trees—ancient, sprawling, near-immortal. To your eyes they might just be trees. But to the biologist, they are something far stranger: living mathematicians.

Each tree releases its fruit not randomly, but according to the Fibonacci sequence, optimizing the number of figs per cycle to match the feeding patterns of bats and birds. The tree does not have a brain, yet it calculates the perfect moment to sustain its ecosystem.

The acacia, another silent genius, has evolved to communicate using chemical signals—warning nearby trees when predators arrive. When a giraffe chews on its leaves, the acacia releases ethylene gas, triggering neighboring trees to pump their own leaves with bitter tannins. A tree anticipating an attack. A forest communicating through chemical codes.

Life is not mechanical. It is intentional.

Case Study III: The Brain That Predicts the Future

In 2011, neuroscientists at the Max Planck Institute for Human Cognitive and Brain Sciences conducted a study that rattled the foundations of free will. Using fMRI scans, they found that a human brain "decides" an action up to 7 seconds before the person becomes aware of it. Before you even think you've made a choice, your neurons have already fired the necessary electrical patterns to execute it.

Your brain is not just a machine of memory—it is a machine of foresight. It predicts what you will do before you do it. It anticipates words before you speak them. It sees the future before you even realize it exists.

The universe is a book written in patterns. The question is not whether you can read it. The question is whether you are willing to unlearn what they taught you—and start seeing the hidden script behind reality. *"Because to create is to see. To see is to know."*

And to know—truly know—is to understand that science and art were never separate to begin with. They were simply different

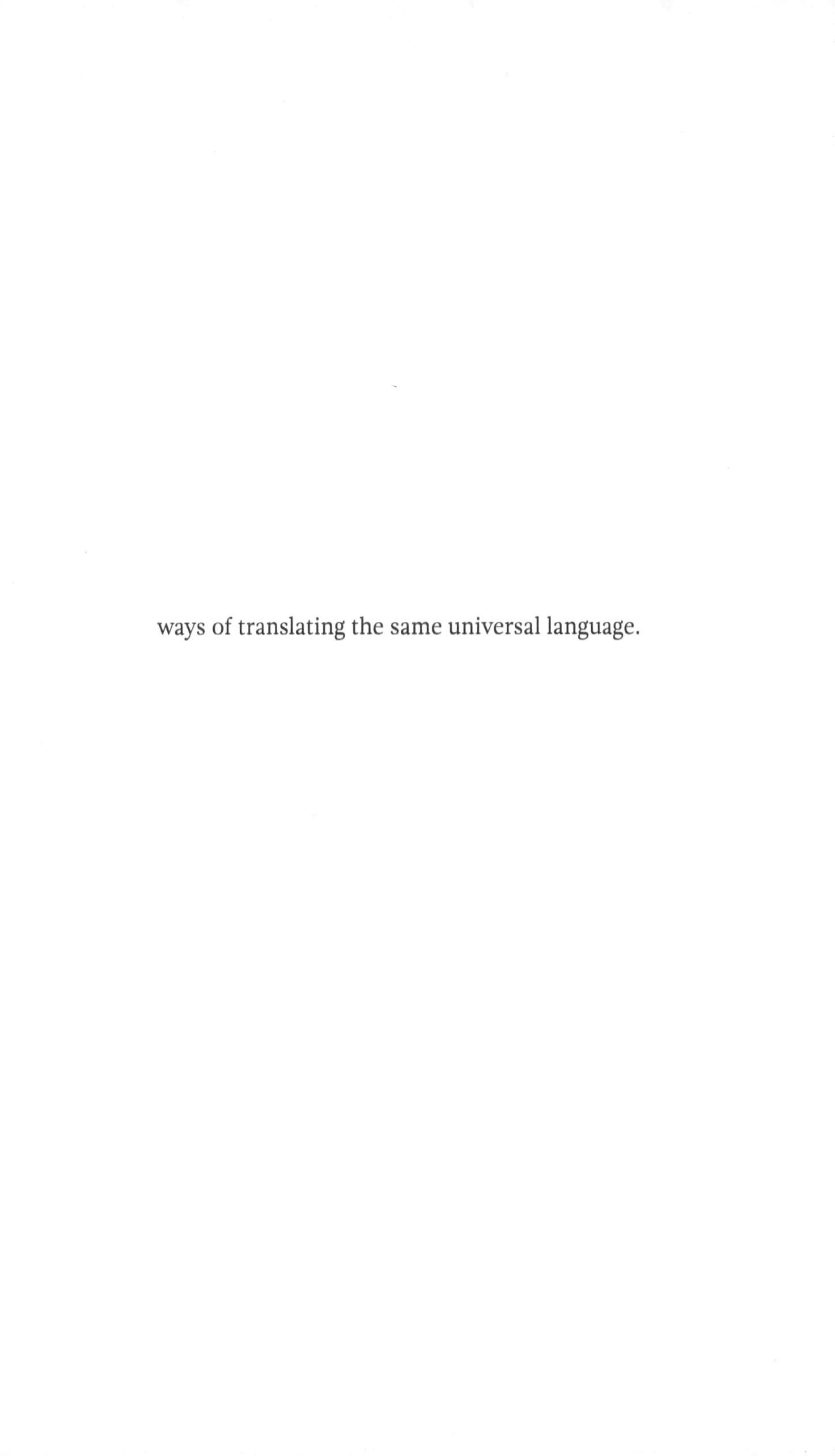

ways of translating the same universal language.

The Architect of Reality

You were told that reality is solid. That what you see is what exists. But what if i say you were lied . You do not see the world as it is. You see it as your brain allows you to.

Case Study I: The Eyes That Edit Reality

In 1999, researchers at Harvard conducted the now-famous "Invisible Gorilla" experiment. Participants were asked to watch a video and count how many times a group of players passed a basketball. Halfway through the video, a man in a full-body gorilla suit walked across the screen, pausing briefly before leaving.

Nearly 50% of the participants never saw him.

The reason? Selective attention. Your brain prioritizes patterns over raw data. It edits reality in real-time, deciding what is "important" and what is "noise." This means you are not seeing the full picture of the world around you—only the version your mind deems necessary. If a gorilla can walk through your vision unnoticed, what else are you blind to?

Case Study II: The Woman Who Felt No Pain

Jo Cameron, a retired teacher from Scotland, lived for 65 years without realizing she was different. She had never felt physical pain.She only discovered this when doctors attempted to treat her for severe arthritis—only to find that she had no need for painkillers. Geneticists at University College London later discovered the reason: a mutation in her FAAH-OUT gene, which controls pain reception and stress response. Her body did not perceive pain. Her brain did not register fear. This mutation could one day be engineered into others—eliminating suffering at the molecular level. But the larger truth is more unsettling: Pain, fear, stress—these are not absolute realities. They are biochemical codes.

And codes can be rewritten.

Case Study III: The Heart That Remembers

Science tells you that memories reside in the brain. That your experiences are stored in the neural pathways of your mind. But what if that is not exactly true ?

In 2008, a woman named Claire Sylvia received a heart transplant from an 18-year-old boy who had died in a motorcycle accident. After her surgery, something strange happened. She craved foods she had never liked before. She had dreams of a man she had never met. Upon meeting the boy's family, she discovered that the cravings matched his favorite foods. The dreams resembled his last moments. Doctors dismissed it as coincidence. But dozens of similar cases exist—organ recipients experiencing new preferences, memories, even personality shifts. Could memory exist beyond the brain? Could identity reside not in neurons, but in cells themselves? If so, the line between self and other, mind and body, memory and matter—begins to blur. You were taught to believe in absolutes. That pain is inevitable, that vision is truth, that memory belongs to the brain.

But pain is a switch. Vision is selective. Memory is fluid.Reality is not fixed.It is constructed.And those who understand this—who know how to shape perception, rewrite pain, and store memory in more than just the mind—will become the true architects of reality.

The Code of Flesh

You believe your body is yours. That it is singular, complete, and solely yours to command. But you are not one being. You are an ecosystem. A walking, breathing collaboration of trillions of separate entities.

Case Study I: The Parasite That Controls Minds

Deep in the Amazon, a fungus known as Ophiocordyceps unilateralis infects carpenter ants, invading their nervous system. The ant, once in control of its own body, suddenly stops thinking for itself.It climbs to a precise height of 25 centimeters—where temperature and humidity are perfect for fungal growth. Then, it clamps its mandibles onto a leaf and waits. The fungus kills it from within, then erupts from its skull—releasing spores to infect the next host. Fascinating right ?

The question is , If a mere fungus can hijack a nervous system, forcing its host to act against its will—*how much of your own behavior is truly your own?*

Case Study II: The Bacteria That Shapes Your Desires

In 2014, researchers at the California Institute of Technology made a startling discovery.Your gut bacteria can influence your cravings, emotions, and even decisions. Certain strains of Lactobacillus increase serotonin production, affecting mood. Bacteroides influence dopamine levels. Some bacteria even secrete neuroactive compounds that alter brain function. In essence, the trillions of microbes inside you are negotiating what you eat, how you feel, and perhaps even what you want. Are you craving chocolate, or is your microbiome demanding sugar for its own survival?

Are you making choices, or are you a vessel for microscopic dictators?

Case Study III: The Blood That Remembers

A study conducted at Stanford University found that injecting young blood into old mice reversed cognitive decline and increased muscle strength. Age-related diseases began to reverse. The elderly mice became faster, stronger, and mentally sharper—simply because young blood circulated through their veins. The implications were disturbing. Could aging be slowed—or even reversed—by something as simple as transfusion? And if so, what happens when this knowledge falls into the hands of those who seek power over death itself ? Your body is not your own. It is a battleground of microbes, a machine that can be reprogrammed. What does this mean? It means control is an illusion. But those who understand the illusion can manipulate it. Rewriting the self is possible. Not through belief. Not through willpower.

But through understanding the code beneath the flesh.

Rewrite the Flesh

You believe your body is static. That your DNA is fixed from birth, dictating your height, intelligence, and even your fate. But what if you could rewrite yourself? I wondered the same question .What if biology was not a prison, but a script—*one you could edit*?

Case Study I: The Boy Who Regrew His Finger

In 2005, a man named Lee Spievack, a hobby pilot, accidentally severed the tip of his finger in a propeller accident. Doctors told him he would never regrow it.But his brother, a scientist, had access to something unusual: powdered extracellular matrix from a pig's bladder.He sprinkled it onto the wound.Within weeks, something miraculous happened: Spievack's fingertip began regenerating. Skin, nerves, even the nail grew back as if it had never been lost.

This wasn't science fiction. During that time it emerged ,it happened ,but then it was taken away from the sight of the mass. After asking him , he didnt give a clear answer. But if this was true then it was bio-scaffolding—tissue engineering at a molecular level.

Case Study II: The Woman Who Changed Her Own DNA

In 2017, a Harvard researcher named Josiah Zayner injected himself with CRISPR gene-editing technology. But the true revolution wasn't in a lab—it was in China. There, a woman with a life-threatening blood disease became the first human to have her genes permanently rewritten using CRISPR.The result? She was cured. With a single molecular tool, she became a different genetic entity. DNA was no longer destiny. It was code. And code can be rewritten.

Case Study III: The Man Who Became Two

In 2019, a bone marrow transplant was performed on a leukemia patient. But something bizarre happened. Months later, DNA tests showed that his blood was no longer his own. His genetic identity had been completely replaced by the donor's DNA. Even the DNA in his saliva and semen had changed. Legally, biologically—he was two people at once. This was more than medicine. It was a shift in what it means to be human. You were told that your body defines you. That you are your DNA. That your limits are set. But limits are a myth.

The flesh can be rewritten. DNA is a canvas. "*The human body is not a final product, it is an evolving script*."And those who understand this will shape the next era of existence.

Beyond Flesh

If biology can be rewritten, what comes next? The next frontier is augmentation—the merging of biology with technology, where flesh is no longer the ultimate form of evolution. What happens when the body is no longer enough?

Case Study I: The Cyborg Who Can Hear Colors

Neil Harbisson was born completely colorblind. He lived in a world of black, white, and gray.But he refused to accept his limitations.He implanted an antenna directly into his skull, a cybernetic extension that translates color frequencies into sound waves. Now, he "hears" colors.Red has a sound. Blue has a frequency. Even ultraviolet and infrared—wavelengths that no human can perceive—are now part of his reality.Harbisson is recognized as the first officially recognized cyborg. His passport photo even includes his antenna.He is not just a human.

He is a hybrid of biology and machine.

Case Study II: The Man Who Feels Magnetic Fields

In 2005, a body modification enthusiast known as "Lepht Anonym" implanted rare earth magnets under his skin.At first, it seemed trivial—a parlor trick.But soon, something changed. His brain adapted. The magnets began picking up electromagnetic fields from everyday devices—he could feel microwaves, sense Wi-Fi signals, and detect the presence of electronics in a room.His nervous system had expanded.This was no longer just a modification—it was a new sense.

Case Study III: The Biocompatible Revolution

Biotechnology companies are racing to push these ideas further. The North Sense Project created small implants that allow humans to physically sense the Earth's magnetic field—like birds and sharks. Elon Musk's Neuralink is attempting to create brain-machine interfaces that could allow thought-controlled devices, enhanced memory, and even direct mind-to-mind communication. And beyond them, researchers are developing bionic limbs that move by thought, synthetic eyes that grant infrared vision, and nanotech that repairs cells from within.

You were told that your body is the peak of evolution.But the truth is your body is just the beginning.The next step isn't just to rewrite biology. It is to transcend it. The future belongs to those who refuse to remain helpless humans succumed to the despair of life and to evolve into something greater .

The Death of Death

What if aging wasn't inevitable? What if death wasn't the end—but a flaw in the system waiting to be fixed?For centuries, humans have accepted mortality as fate. But today, scientists, biohackers, and billionaires are challenging death itself.

Case Study I: The Jellyfish That Lives Forever

Deep in the ocean, there exists a creature that never dies.Turritopsis dohrnii, a small jellyfish, has a secret: when it reaches the end of its life cycle, it doesn't decay. Instead, it reverts its cells back to a juvenile state, starting its life all over again. This process, known as biological immortality, means this jellyfish could theoretically live forever.Now, scientists are studying how to apply this regenerative ability to human cells.

Case Study II: The Man with the Youngest Blood

Billionaire tech moguls have invested millions into parabiosis—the transfusion of young blood into older bodies. One of the most controversial figures is Bryan Johnson, a biohacker who spends over $2 million annually on anti-aging research. He undergoes plasma transfusions from his teenage son, claiming it slows down his biological clock. Early experiments on mice showed that old mice given young blood became biologically younger—their muscles strengthened, their brains sharpened.

The question is: will this work on humans?

Case Study III: The First Cryogenically Frozen Human

In 1967, a psychology professor named James Bedford died of cancer. But instead of being buried, he became the first human to be cryogenically frozen. His body still lies in a steel chamber filled with liquid nitrogen, waiting for a future where science can revive the dead. Today, cryonics facilities house hundreds of frozen bodies, with some companies even offering to preserve just the brain—on the belief that future AI could restore a person's consciousness in a digital form.

The War on Aging: Science or Hubris?

From genetic engineering to AI-driven medicine, we are racing toward a future where aging is a disease that can be treated. Harvard scientists have reversed aging in mice using gene therapy. Metformin, a diabetes drug, is being tested as an anti-aging pill for humans. Altos Labs, a biotech company backed by Jeff Bezos, is researching cell reprogramming to extend human lifespan. But if we conquer aging... what comes next?

Will immortality be a privilege of the rich? Will a world without death lead to overpopulation?And if humans can live forever... should they? This is not just science fiction. It is a question of ethics, identity, and the soul. Because when you take away death... you change what it means to be human.

The Digital Afterlife

If the mind is just electrical signals and data, then can it be copied, stored, and transferred like a computer file? Some believe true immortality isn't about preserving the body, *it's about preserving the self.*

Case Study I: The Man Who 'Lives' After Death

In 2023, a man named Roman Mazurenko died in an accident. But his friend, a tech developer, refused to let go. She trained an AI chatbot using thousands of his text messages, creating a digital Roman—a bot that spoke, joked, and responded just like he did. Was it really him? Or just a machine mimicking his patterns?

Now, companies like Replika AI and Project December offer people the chance to create digital clones of themselves before they die—so loved ones can talk to them even after they're gone.

Case Study II: The Silicon Mind of Nectome

A controversial startup named Nectome is working on a way to preserve human brains at the moment of death, freezing neural connections in perfect detail. Their theory? One day, scientists will be able to map every neuron and recreate a person's consciousness inside a machine. They call it "brain emulation."

Imagine waking up in a digital world, your memories intact—but without a body. Would that still be you?

The AI Resurrection: Can a Machine Hold a Soul?

Some researchers believe the key isn't copying the brain, but training an AI to become you. AI models could learn your speech, your emotions, your decision-making patterns.Your entire personality could be simulated. Some predict that future AI will allow people to interact with long-dead historical figures, reconstructed from their writings. But does a digital version of you count as you? Or is it just a ghost in the machine?

Merging With Machines: The Road to Transhumanism

Rather than copying minds, some scientists believe the solution is to merge with AI. Elon Musk's Neuralink is working on brain implants that will let humans interface directly with computers. Scientists predict that by 2045, human consciousness could be enhanced by AI, blending thought and technology.

A future where you don't just think... you compute.But if we become part AI, part human... where do we draw the line? *Are we still ourselves?* And only then we may start to reconsider art into our life .

If parts of our brain become coded software, we have to ask: who are we then? Some theorists argue consciousness could survive as pure informationphilarchive.org, but critics warn that making a perfect digital copy of your brain pattern would leave you facing a duplicate, not the original selfphilarchive.org. In such a world, one thing might keep us anchored: *art*. Imagination and creativity born of our deepest emotions and struggles , the uniquely human drive for meaning could become more essential than ever, something machines can mimic in skill but never truly feel.

Another You

The thought of this haunting yet amusing right ? If your entire mind could be copied and uploaded into a machine, would you still need a biological body? Or could science build you a new one?

Case Study I: The First Cloned Mammal—Dolly the Sheep

In 1996, Dolly the sheep became the first mammal ever cloned from an adult cell. The experiment proved that DNA could be used to create an identical living being. Since then, scientists have cloned cows,pigs, and even monkeys .
Some researchers now ask: Can we clone humans next?

Case Study II: The Billionaire Betting on Rebirth

Russian tech mogul Dmitry Itskov has a radical dream .By 2045, he believes humans will no longer need biological bodies. His project, called The 2045 Initiative, is funding research to,transfer human minds into synthetic bodies .Create humanoid robots powered by real human consciousness .Achieve "digital reincarnation". He predicts that in the future, people will buy designer bodies—choosing their ideal age, strength, and appearance.

A new form of immortality.

Case Study III: Can We Print a Human?

Scientists have already 3D-printed human organs—hearts, kidneys, even skin. Some researchers now propose using stem cells and bioprinting to create fully functional human bodies. The idea? If your original body fails, just grow a new one. But if you wake up in a cloned body with your memories intact... are you still the same person? Or just a copy?

The Ethics of Rebuilding Humans

The idea of cloning and synthetic bodies raises deep ethical concerns, If someone clones themselves, who owns the identity? If wealthy elites can replace their bodies, will only the rich live forever? If we stop aging, what happens to natural evolution? Can i share one more secret with you ? Well some conspiracy theories believe that this is already happening , how ,where ,when ..... all this is still a secret for me .

For centuries, humans have accepted the body as part of the self. But science is challenging that idea. What if the future is not about living longer, but about never needing a body at all?
Can you imagine such a world mentioned above and we are disconneted from art then what will be the consequences ? If we (the ones who see art and science as one) dont step forward into these fields then what the possibilites of horror that could happen ?

Playing God

Throughout history, every civilization has told cautionary tales about those who tried to defy nature—those who created life, sought immortality, or tampered with the laws of existence. But in the 21st century, these aren't myths anymore. They are reality.

Case Study I: He Created Life—Then Destroyed It

In 2010, scientist Craig Venter did the impossible. He created the first synthetic life form—a bacterium with DNA completely designed by humans. This lifeform—called Synthia—had a watermark in its genetic code that read:
"To live, to err, to fall, to triumph, and to create life out of life."
But soon after its success, Synthia was destroyed. Why? Some feared that artificial life could evolve beyond human control. What if synthetic organisms, mutated into something unstoppable? Developed self-awareness? Became a new form of intelligence—one that doesn't need humans? Venter proved that creating life isn't a dream anymore. It's a choice.

Case Study II: The Scientist Who Edited Babies

In 2018, Chinese scientist He Jiankui made a shocking announcement,he had genetically edited human embryos to make them resistant to HIV. The first genetically modified babies were born—two twin girls.At first, people saw it as a breakthrough. Then, they realized the consequences, If we can edit one trait, what stops us from designing humans? Will the rich create genetically superior bloodlines? If intelligence, beauty, and strength become programmable, what happens to natural humanity?

He Jiankui was arrested. His research was banned. But the Pandora's Box has been opened—other scientists are still secretly experimenting with genetic modifications.

The Danger of Perfecting Life

The desire to improve, enhance, and perfect is natural. But history has shown that the pursuit of ultimate control over life always comes with a cost. The Nazis conducted horrific genetic experiments to create a "superior race." The Soviet Union tried to breed humans with apes to make stronger soldiers.The Manhattan Project led to nuclear bombs—designed for peace, but used for war. At what point does scientific advancement become playing God?

If we create life... do we also have the right to destroy it?

Architects of Evolution

We like to believe that evolution is random—that nature is the sole artist, sculpting life through time. But what if evolution has been... guided? What if the greatest transformations in biology were not purely natural but the result of hidden hands—ancient and modern—intervening in ways we do not understand?

Case Study I: The Cambrian Explosion—A Sudden Leap in Evolution

550 million years ago, something impossible happened. For 3 billion years, life on Earth was simple—microscopic bacteria, algae, and a few soft-bodied creatures. Then, within a geological blink of an eye (less than 10 million years), nature suddenly invented complexity - Eyes with lenses, Exoskeletons and advanced nervous systems ,Predators and prey—an instant arms race of intelligence, Fossils show no transitional forms. No slow, gradual shift—just an explosion of fully formed creatures.

Even Darwin himself was disturbed by this. He called it "a mystery" that could shatter his theory.Some scientists speculate,was there an unknown force accelerating evolution? Did ancient biological engineers exist far before humans? Or did life itself possess a hidden intelligence, unlocking its own potential?

Case Study II: The Human Brain—An Unnatural Evolution?

Something even stranger happened 2 million years ago—our brains tripled in size. Evolution never moves this fast. It takes millions of years for a species to change significantly. But for humans, intelligence didn't just evolve—it exploded. Biology cannot fully explain,why human neural connections grew at an extreme rate ? Why we developed abstract thought and self-awareness something no other species achieved? Why the human brain, which requires enormous energy, was favored by evolution when nature usually prefers efficiency ?

The controversial question that arises here is that ,
Did humans naturally evolve intelligence... or was something guiding our development?

The Hidden Hands of Biological Engineering

If evolution is a design, then who—or what—is designing it? Modern science is now playing the same game. CRISPR gene editing allows us to rewrite human DNA. Artificial intelligence may soon merge with biology, creating hybrid minds. The dream of immortality is being actively pursued by billionaires in secret labs. If humans are now engineering life, what does that say about our own past? Were we, too, a creation?

And if we create the next version of life, will it still be... human?

CHAPTER THREE

VELUM

(The Veil of Reality: Unraveling the Code of Art and Science)
"To see beyond is to unmake the illusion."

The Hidden Codes in Art

Art has always fascinated me—not just for its beauty but for the way it hides things in plain sight. I can't shake the feeling that some of the greatest works in history weren't just artistic expressions but messages, waiting for the right minds to decode them.

Take Leonardo da Vinci. Everyone talks about him like he was just a painter, but come on—he was so much more. The man designed machines we still struggle to build today, sketched anatomical structures with insane accuracy, and then... left us a collection of art that, when looked at closely, seems to whisper secrets no one can quite hear.

The Last Supper—A Song Hidden in a Painting?

I came across this theory a while back, and it still sends chills down my spine. A musician once analyzed The Last Supper and found that if you overlay musical notes on the way the hands and loaves of bread are positioned, they actually form a melody. Think about that. A painting that plays music.

The theory suggests that Leonardo da Vinci may have hidden a musical composition in The Last Supper. An Italian musician, Giovanni Maria Pala, discovered that the hands of the apostles and the loaves of bread align with musical notes. When played from right to left, just as Leonardo wrote, the notes form a solemn 40-second melody. This idea highlights Leonardo's deep understanding of both art and science, showing how he may have blended music into his masterpiece in a way no one expected.

It's eerie, isn't it? It makes me wonder, was da Vinci just playing around? Or was he encoding something only certain minds would understand? And if he did it with music, what else did he hide?

The Last Supper by Leonardo da Vinci

The Vitruvian Man—A Blueprint for Something Bigger?

Everyone's seen *The Vitruvian Man*, that famous sketch of a man with his arms outstretched, inside a perfect circle and square. We all learned it's about proportions, but there's something deeper going on.

What's even more fascinating is how the drawing seems to foreshadow modern bioengineering principles. The symmetry and proportions of the Vitruvian Man mirror the fractal-like patterns found in nature, patterns that we now understand play a crucial role in cell division, genetic coding, and artificial intelligence modeling. Some researchers even speculate that da Vinci, centuries ahead of his time, intuitively grasped concepts of biomechanics and biorobotics,ideas that are only now being explored in fields like cybernetics and transhumanism.. The question is: How did he know?

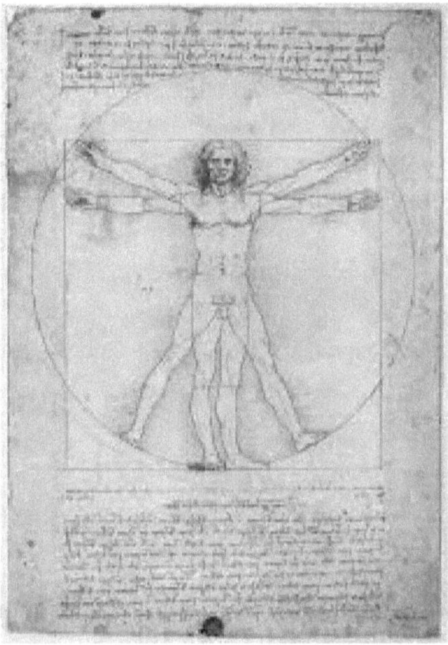

The Vitruvian Man

Michelangelo and the Hidden Brain in the Sistine Chapel

Such a beautiful painting that made me decide to buy one . Michelangelo was another one of those minds who saw the world differently. When I first learned that his painting of God giving life to Adam perfectly outlines the shape of a human brain, I felt this strange sense of realization—almost like I was seeing through a trick that had fooled humanity for centuries.

A neuroscientist discovered this in the 1990s. If you overlay the image of the human brain onto that part of the Sistine Chapel, everything, down to the folds and the brainstem, matches up.And that's when it hit me: Was Michelangelo hinting at something? That intelligence, our mind, our ability to think—*is the real divine power?* That maybe, just maybe, ***God wasn't a being in the clouds, but the very consciousness inside us?***

If that's true, why did he hide it inside a religious painting? Was it because speaking these ideas outright would have been dangerous?And if that's the case—how much more knowledge was hidden because the world wasn't ready for it?

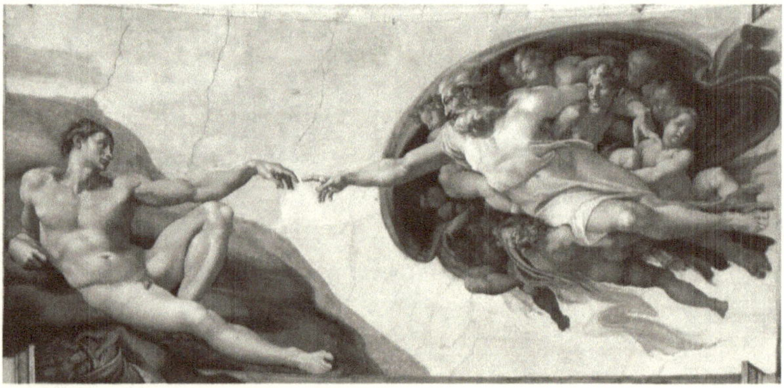

Sistine Chapel

The Twist—What Else Have We Overlooked?

The more I dig into this, the more I realize that history isn't just what's been recorded, *it's what's been erased.* Da Vinci. Michelangelo. Even ancient Egyptian artists who carved mysterious hieroglyphs that resemble modern aircraft... all of them left behind clues. Clues that don't fit the timeline we've been given. So I have to ask,

Are there more hidden codes we haven't cracked yet? Did these artists know things that would've rewritten history? And most importantly—who were they trying to keep this knowledge from? Because maybe... just maybe... the real secret isn't what they left behind. *It's what they never let us find.*

The Lost Knowledge of Ancient Civilizations

History has always been written by the victors. But what about the ones who lost? What about the knowledge that was burned, buried, or deliberately erased? The more I search, the more I see a pattern, *every civilization that reached a certain level of understanding mysteriously collapsed.* What if they knew something that made them too powerful? What if we were never meant to remember what they discovered?

The Library of Alexandria—A Knowledge Massacre

The Library of Alexandria was more than just a collection of books—it was a powerhouse of knowledge, a center where scholars from all over the world gathered to study medicine, astronomy, engineering, and even the secrets of human consciousness. Then one day, it was burned. We're told it was an accident, a casualty of war. But I don't buy it. The Romans, the Christians, the Muslims—every power that ruled over Alexandria had a reason to control that library.

The real question is: What was in those scrolls that made them worth destroying?

Some say they contained blueprints for advanced technology—machines that ran on energy we still don't understand. Others believe they held the key to immortality, secret formulas lost forever in the flames. And then there's the theory that among those scrolls were documents explaining how to control human thought itself. And that makes me wonder—what if someone did manage to keep those secrets?

What if they never truly disappeared, just went underground?

The Mysterious Case of the Baghdad Battery

In 1938, a German archaeologist unearthed something that shouldn't have existed, a clay jar with an iron rod and a copper cylinder inside. When tested, scientists found that if filled with an acidic liquid like vinegar, it could generate electricity. This wasn't a modern invention. This was found in ancient Iraq, dating back to 200 BC. How? Who was using it? And for what?

Historians dismiss it as a coincidence, arguing that it wasn't used for electricity in the way we understand today. Yet, evidence suggests that ancient civilizations may have harnessed energy through methods beyond our current comprehension. Their understanding of power and science may have followed an entirely different paradigm, one that defies conventional theories and hints at lost knowledge hidden within history's depths.

The Biochemical Science of the Mayans—Did They Crack Genetic Engineering?

The Mayans weren't just brilliant architects; they were scientists in ways we rarely acknowledge. Their knowledge of plants, medicine, and even genetics was shockingly advanced. Some of their carvings depict humans with animal-like features, leading some researchers to speculate that they might have experimented with early forms of genetic modification. They selectively bred plants to produce new species—corn didn't exist naturally; they made it. Their shamans used hallucinogenic substances that seem to trigger higher states of consciousness, almost like unlocking parts of the brain modern neuroscience is only beginning to study. Some ancient Mayan skulls show signs of cranial modification, which eerily resembles the elongated skulls found in Egypt and

Peru.

What were they trying to achieve? Enhanced intelligence? Stronger, faster humans? And why did these practices disappear so suddenly?

The Twist—A Pattern of Erasure

Here's what keeps me up at night, The Library of Alexandria burned ,The Mayan civilization vanished ,The Baghdad Battery ignored,Da Vinci's inventions hidden,Nikola Tesla's blueprints confiscated ,It's not just lost knowledge. It's a pattern.

A pattern that suggests knowledge isn't lost by accident, *it's erased when it becomes too powerful.*So the real question isn't just what they knew...It's who decided we shouldn't know it.

Secret of having a Human mind

For centuries, we've been told that the human brain is an enigma, a complex yet mostly understood machine. But the deeper I look, the more I realize—*we are nowhere close to understanding the true capabilities of our own minds*. Some people see the world differently. They create beyond their time, they perceive things others cannot. We call them geniuses, prophets, mystics, but what if they simply unlocked a part of the brain that the rest of us cannot access?

And what if we were never meant to?

The Case of Savants—The Hidden Codes in Our Brains

There are people among us who defy every rule of human intelligence. Take Daniel Tammet, for example, a man who can recite 22,514 digits of Pi from memory and learn an entirely new language in a week. Or Kim Peek, the inspiration behind Rain Man, who could read two pages of a book at the same time, one with each eye. Their brains are wired differently, yes. But what if that's the original design? What if the rest of us have simply been conditioned to forget?

Scientific studies have shown that savants may have access to raw, unfiltered data processing, something our conscious minds cannot normally tap into. The brain has neural inhibitors, mechanisms that actually prevent us from accessing certain information too fast. But why? Some theorists believe that human intelligence has been deliberately limited over time, that these "mental locks" were not an accident but a necessity, to keep society controllable, predictable.

If every person could memorize entire libraries, process mathematical patterns instantly, or even see beyond the limits of normal perception, how would the world function? Who would be in power?***What if true genius is not rare,but suppressed?***

Nikola Tesla and the Visionaries Who Claimed to See Beyond

Tesla spoke of ideas that came to him in flashes, visions so vivid that he could see his inventions before even drawing them. He once wrote, "*My brain is only a receiver, in the Universe there is a core from which we obtain knowledge, strength, and inspiration.*" He believed that knowledge was not something we create, but something we tap into. A frequency, a signal,one that very few could access.

But Tesla wasn't alone in this.Edgar Cayce, a renowned psychic, claimed to have entered a trance state where he could diagnose illnesses and prescribe cures with no prior medical training.Srinivasa Ramanujan, the mathematical prodigy from India, said that the formulas he discovered were revealed to him in dreams by a divine entity.Goethe, the famous writer, described an experience where he suddenly saw another version of himself, dressed in different clothes, walking past him in broad daylight—an event some later described as a glitch in reality itself.

What if their minds were accessing a deeper level of reality—one that is normally hidden from us?

The Science of Consciousness—A Hidden Mechanism in the Brain?

Neuroscience tells us that human beings use only a fraction of their brain's true potential. But here's something they don't emphasize enough—There is a structure inside your brain called the pineal gland. Some call it the "third eye," and for good reason.

It contains light-sensitive cells, just like your actual eyes.It produces DMT, a compound linked to intense spiritual and out-of-body experiences. Ancient civilizations from Egypt to India revered it as the seat of higher consciousness.

But here's where it gets disturbing.In modern times, our pineal glands are calcified , coated in layers of fluoride and environmental toxins. Scientists call it harmless, a byproduct of modern living. But some researchers believe this is intentional, a way to keep the human brain from reaching its full awareness.

Why would that matter? Because the pineal gland is believed to regulate perception, intuition, and even time itself. If this gland were truly activated, would we be able to see reality for what it actually is?

And if so... who benefits from keeping it suppressed?

The Twist—What If Everything We Know About Intelligence Is a Lie?

If intelligence is not just genetic but something that can be unlocked, why do schools not teach us how?
If higher states of awareness are possible, why do most people never experience them?
If consciousness itself is more than just neurons firing, why do we keep pretending it isn't?

I believe there is a reason why knowledge is hidden. Not because we cannot understand it, but because if we did, *the world would change overnight*.Somewhere, someone benefits from keeping us small.And that is exactly why I refuse to stop asking questions.

The Science of Energy

We have been told that we are flesh and bone, that our thoughts are electrical signals, that our emotions are merely chemical reactions. But what if that is only part of the truth?

Modern science tells us that everything, *everything*, is made of energy. Matter, in its most fundamental form, is nothing more than vibrating energy fields. Even solid objects, like your desk or your own body, are just clusters of atoms held together by invisible forces. So why do we still see the world as rigid, unchanging? Because our minds are trained to.

But what happens when we look deeper?

The Hidden Truth of Bioelectricity

In the 18th century, an Italian scientist named Luigi Galvani discovered something shocking—when he touched a dead frog's leg with a metal instrument, it moved. The discovery of bioelectricity changed medicine forever. But here's what they don't tell you: Every human cell generates electricity. The human heart has a magnetic field that extends several feet beyond the body. The brain emits frequencies—patterns that can be recorded, even altered.In other words, we are not just biological machines. *We are conductors of energy, walking power sources with electromagnetic signatures unique to each of us.*

Ancient traditions have long believed that human beings have an "aura," an invisible energy field that affects our health, emotions, and even the way we interact with the world. Science now backs this up, Kirlian photography has captured electrical discharges around living beings, and researchers have measured distinct changes in a person's electromagnetic field based on their mood, health, and even thoughts.

If our thoughts create electrical impulses, and electricity affects matter, then...Can thoughts shape reality itself?

The Double-Slit Experiment—Does Consciousness Create Reality?

One of the strangest experiments in quantum physics is the double-slit experiment. It proves something mind-bending-Particles behave differently when they are being observed.When scientists fire tiny particles (like electrons) at a barrier with two slits, the particles behave like waves passing through both slits at once. But the moment they place an observer to watch what's happening, the particles start behaving like solid objects, picking only one path.

Consciousness changes the outcome.What does this mean? *It suggests that reality itself is not fixed—"it responds to observation."* Some physicists, including Nobel Prize winners like Eugene Wigner, have even proposed that reality does not exist independently of the observer. In other words...*The world may not be as objective as we think.*

This aligns with what many ancient traditions have said for thousands of years—*that human consciousness is not just a passive receiver of information but an active creator of reality.*

Case Study: The Placebo Effect—The Brain's Power to Heal Itself

Let's look at a real-world example of the mind influencing reality—the placebo effect.Patients given fake pills (that contain no actual medicine) have been shown to heal from illnesses just because they believe they are receiving real treatment. People injected with saline solutions instead of painkillers have reported complete pain relief—simply because their brains expected the effect. In some studies, even fake surgeries have led to patients recovering from serious conditions.

How is this possible?Science says it's because the brain releases chemicals like endorphins and dopamine, mimicking the effect of real medicine. But if the brain can heal the body just by believing in the cure, doesn't that imply that belief itself is a force that shapes reality?If the mind can influence health, why stop there? What else could it influence? *Money? Success? Fate?*

If we are constantly broadcasting electrical signals into the world... what if reality is simply responding to us?

The Twist—What If Reality Is a Mirror?

What if everything we see around us is a reflection—not just of the physical world, but of the energy we emit?The ancient Hermetic principles teach that *"As above, so below. As within, so without."* Meaning, the universe is a reflection of the self. Modern psychology calls this confirmation bias—we notice things that match our beliefs and ignore what doesn't.

But what if it's more than just a psychological trick?What if reality is literally adjusting itself based on our mental and energetic state?Why do some people seem to attract success effortlessly, while others struggle for years? Why do certain individuals walk into a room and command attention without saying a word?Why do lucky people always seem to be in the right place at the right time? Maybe it's not just luck. Maybe they've tapped into something deeper.An unspoken law of energy, perception, and belief. If this is true, then the biggest secret of all is this: *You are not a passive observer of life. You are its architect.*

And once you understand this, you can never see the world the same way again.

Science of Symbols

Since the dawn of civilization, symbols have carried knowledge that words often fail to express. They have guided rulers, inspired revolutions, and held secrets known only to a few. From the intricate carvings of ancient temples to the corporate logos we see every day, symbols are not just decoration—they are carriers of power, intention, and influence.

But what if symbols are not just cultural artifacts? What if they tap into something much deeper—something wired into the human mind itself?

The Biology of Symbols—Why Our Brain Responds to Them

Our brains process symbols faster than language. Before we could write, before we could even speak fluently, early humans used symbols to communicate. Even today: A red light means stop, a green light means go. A skull and crossbones trigger an instinct of danger.A heart shape immediately suggests love.This is not just learned behavior—it's wired into us.

Case Study: The Eye and the Mind

Neurologists have found that certain shapes and patterns activate subconscious parts of the brain. The human eye is naturally drawn to spirals, geometric patterns, and sacred proportions like the Fibonacci sequence. That's why ancient architects—from the Egyptians to the Greeks—designed temples, palaces, and even entire cities based on mathematical symbols. These patterns, like the Golden Ratio (1.618), appear in nature, from the spirals of galaxies to the arrangement of sunflower seeds. The human face, when considered "perfectly beautiful," often aligns with this ratio.

So, for me it isn't just aesthetic preference that led ancient civilizations to these patterns. Perhaps they understand something deeper about how symbols affect energy, perception, and even human behavior.

The Symbols of Power—What They Don't Teach You in School

Many of the most influential people in history—scientists, rulers, and artists—were obsessed with symbols. But not just any symbols—symbols of power Take Leonardo da Vinci. Everyone knows him as an artist, but few realize he was deeply involved in sacred geometry. His most famous drawing, Vitruvian Man, was not just about human proportions—it was about the connection between man and the universe. The square represents the material world, the circle represents the divine, and where the human body aligns with both? That's where knowledge meets creation.

Or consider the Ankh, the Egyptian symbol of life. It appears everywhere in ancient texts, often held by gods and pharaohs. Modern researchers now believe it may have been more than just a spiritual emblem—some claim its shape could have been designed to channel energy, like a tuning fork for the human body's bioelectric field.

And then there's the Helix—the double spiral seen in DNA, nature, and even ancient sculptures. Why did civilizations that had no way of seeing molecules still carve spirals into their temples and artifacts? Could they have sensed something about the nature of life itself?

What if symbols were not just abstract ideas but real forces—tools that can be used to influence the mind and shape reality?

Modern Science: The Power of Shape and Thought

Let's look at the Placebo Effect again, but this time in relation to symbols.Researchers found that people given round pills had different reactions than those given square pills—even when they contained the same ingredients.Soft, circular shapes are associated with calmness, while sharp, angular shapes trigger alertness and aggression.Advertisers carefully choose fonts, colors, and logos that subconsciously make you trust or desire a product. In short, *symbols don't just represent meaning—they create it.*

If corporations and governments carefully design symbols to influence people, imagine what understanding the right symbols could do for you.Could symbols affect your success? Could they change your energy? Could they be the key to unlocking a deeper reality? *What if they already are—but only a select few understand how to use them?*

The Twist: You See Symbols Every Day—But Do You Know What They Really Mean?

Think about the logos of some of the world's most powerful companies: The Apple logo—an ancient symbol of knowledge and temptation.The Google 'G'—a perfect spiral, reminiscent of the Golden Ratio.The Mercedes-Benz star—representing domination over land, sea, and air. These are not random choices. They are modern sigils, consciously designed to influence how we think, feel, and behave.

The same principle applies to religious symbols, royal crests, and even the arrangement of cities. In Washington, D.C., for example, the street layout is designed around Masonic symbols—interwoven pentagrams, squares, and compass shapes. Coincidence?

Or is there a hidden language of power that most people never learn to read? Maybe symbols are not just reflections of ideas—maybe they are active forces that influence the world, just like words or thoughts.And maybe the greatest secret of all is this,*If you understand the language of symbols, you can rewrite reality itself.*

What They Didn't Want Us to See

Alright, let's get real.There's something about art—something beyond paint on a canvas or words on a page. It's never just art. It's a code, a system of messages wrapped in beauty so that only the right minds catch it. And science? It's not separate from art. The greatest scientists were artists in disguise, hiding knowledge in plain sight.And yet, no one talks about it. No one teaches this in school.

Because if you see it, you start asking the wrong questions. Or maybe the right ones.

The Art That Watches You Back

Have you ever looked at a painting and felt like it was looking back? Not in some supernatural way, but in a way that makes you feel like the artist knew something you don't? Because they did. Take the Mona Lisa. Everyone obsesses over her smile, her mystery—but no one asks why da Vinci painted her in such an unnatural way. The background doesn't align. Her eyes follow you. And the more you look, the more uncomfortable you feel.

Because it's not just a portrait. It's a test. Da Vinci wasn't just an artist—he was an anatomist, an engineer, a scientist who saw things differently. He studied the human body like a machine, understanding how we see, how we perceive, how we think. Mona Lisa isn't about beauty; it's about control. It controls how you look at it.And that's just one example.

Look at Escher's impossible structures, where stairs lead nowhere, bending reality itself. Or Dali's melting clocks, distorting time the way our brains do when we dream.These weren't just paintings. They were studies of perception—tests to see how far the mind can stretch before it breaks.

But here's the real question-If artists figured out how to manipulate perception centuries ago, how much further has modern science taken it?And who's using it now?

Science Was Never Just About Facts

Art is a language. But science? That's where things get deep.Because every great scientist had an obsession with the unseen.*"Science feels dull when reduced to mere calculations for marks, and art seems senseless when viewed without depth."*

Nikola Tesla talked about energy, frequency, and vibration—things we still don't fully understand. Johann Goethe (yes, the poet) secretly discovered how light and darkness weren't just opposites but forces that shaped our perception.Santiago Ramón y Cajal, the father of neuroscience, drew neurons that looked exactly like trees—because everything in nature follows the same patterns.

Patterns. Connections. Everything leads back to the same hidden structures.Take DNA, the building block of life. It's a double helix, a spiral—the same shape seen in galaxies, hurricanes, seashells. The same spiral ancient civilizations carved into their temples, over and over again.

How did they know? How did they understand a shape we only discovered with modern microscopes?Maybe because science isn't about discovery. Maybe it's about remembering what was already known.

The Experiment They Don't Teach You About

Here's something they never mention in textbooks.In the 1980s, a scientist named Jacques Benveniste claimed that water has memory. That it could "remember" substances that had once been in it—even after being diluted beyond detection. Basically, he suggested that water can store information.Sounds like sci-fi, right? But think about this: Our bodies are 70% water. Our planet is mostly water. What if water is more than just a liquid? What if it's a storage device, an unseen recording system for the things it touches?His research was dismissed. He was ridiculed, his career destroyed.

But now, decades later, new studies on quantum coherence in water molecules are bringing his ideas back.What if he was right?What if the human body itself is carrying memories it doesn't even know it has?

The Twist: What Have We Forgotten?

Art hides knowledge. Science rediscovers it. And somewhere between the two, entire generations of understanding have been lost.Or erased.Because imagine if everyone knew-How symbols could change the way we think.How perception could be bent like an optical illusion.How reality itself might not be as solid as we believe.Imagine what that kind of knowledge could do in the wrong hands.

Maybe that's why some of the greatest ideas in history get buried. Why certain scientists and artists end up forgotten.Or maybe...The ones who understood simply chose not to share everything.Maybe they left just enough clues for those who are willing to look deeper.

Are you?

CHAPTER FOUR

Geometriae

(Geometry's Seduction)

"Where symmetry whispers secrets and angles tempt the mind."

Fibonacci's Ghost

Ever heard of golden ratio ? They told you that the golden ratio, that divine proportion of 1.618—was a mathematical curiosity, a quirk of aesthetics, a coincidence found in nature. But was it really?

Look deeper. This pattern does not merely appear in art and architecture. It is the spine of existence. The blueprint of life itself. It whispers through the spiral of galaxies, the arrangement of petals on a flower, the proportions of the human body, even the structure of DNA. Was this truly nature's doing, or was it designed?

The ancient Indians saw it in the sacred Sri Yantra, a geometric mandala whose precise, interlocking triangles are said to contain the secret of the cosmos. The Vedic texts described proportions and harmonics eerily similar to the Fibonacci sequence long before it was 'discovered' in the West. The Brihadeeswara Temple in Tamil Nadu follows a ratio so exact that modern architects still struggle to comprehend its structural perfection. Was this mere intuition, or did they understand something we do not?

And then there are the Ajanta and Ellora caves, sculpted with an almost divine precision. Their layouts align with unseen cosmic energies, the placement of their entrances and the ratios within their halls mirroring the same spiral seen in nautilus shells and galaxies. This was not random. The sages and architects of ancient India knew.

The Ghost of Fibonacci

Leonardo Fibonacci is credited with introducing the famous sequence to the West, but he was merely an observer. The knowledge was always there, lurking in the very fabric of the natural world. The Greeks had it in their Parthenon. The Egyptians embedded it in the Pyramids of Giza, their slopes whispering the divine proportion. Even the Mayan pyramids show the golden ratio in their steps and angles, creating a resonance that echoes through time.

Coincidence? Or something more?

Some physicists now suggest that the Fibonacci sequence might not just be a mathematical curiosity, it could be a fundamental principle of the universe itself, shaping the very way energy moves, the way galaxies spiral, the way reality arranges itself. If that is true, then it means we are all living inside a design—a grand, geometric construct that follows an ancient, hidden order.And yet, the modern world dismisses it. The golden ratio is called a myth, a product of our desire to find patterns where none exist. But if it were just a trick of the mind, why does it keep reappearing in places and structures created centuries apart, in civilizations that never met? Why does the human brain find it irresistibly beautiful?

Now asi sit down to write this , a question strikes my inner conscience . Did nature present us with this proportion, embedding it into our instincts, our perceptions, our very biology? Or is the golden ratio a signature, a mark left behind by *something greater* ? This is not just mathematics. This is the key to reality itself. And if you learn to read the patterns, you will begin to see the world for what it truly is.

"Hidden patterns, unseen truths."

The Hidden Architect—Sacred Geometry

If nature was sculpted by an unseen hand, then geometry is its signature—a silent, precise language woven into the fabric of existence. But who, or what, is the architect of this pattern?

The Temples That Speak in Numbers

Ancient Indian architecture wasn't just about aesthetics. The Vastu Shastra, an ancient Sanskrit manual of architecture, describes how buildings should align with cosmic forces. But here's where it gets strange—the ratios prescribed in these texts often reflect the golden ratio and Fibonacci spirals. The Konark Sun Temple, built as a massive stone chariot, follows proportions that seem to interact with the movement of celestial bodies. The Khajuraho Temples, famous for their intricate carvings, were positioned based on astronomical alignments, their towers resembling the spiraling Fibonacci sequence. Now is this a coincidence ? Perhaps the ancient builders understand something that modern science is only beginning to grasp.

The same patterns appear in Egypt's Great Pyramid, whose slope angle comes astonishingly close to 1.618, and in the Great Mosque of Córdoba, where Islamic architects embedded hidden golden ratios within the arches and domes. Even Da Vinci's Vitruvian Man, often cited as the ultimate example of human proportion, reflects this same mathematical constant.What were they all trying to capture? And why does this same proportion resonate not just in architecture but in life itself?

A Code in Biology? The DNA Spiral and the Phi Connection

Look beyond temples and monuments—this pattern isn't just in stone. It is inside you.Human DNA follows a spiral shape that adheres to Fibonacci ratios. The length of each DNA loop, the very building blocks of life, fits within these ancient proportions. Why? Could it be that life itself was designed to follow this structure, as though guided by an unseen architect? Consider the human body,from the ratio of finger bones to the spacing of facial features, everything aligns mysteriously with the same phi proportion. This is why artists, scientists, and even advertisers unconsciously use it. It feels right to us—*because we are built from it.*

The Fibonacci Spiral in Brainwaves

Neuroscientists have begun studying the brain's response to geometric patterns, and the findings are unsettling. Certain geometric structures—particularly the golden ratio—appear to trigger a harmonic resonance in the brain, leading to enhanced creativity, relaxation, and even altered states of consciousness.Could it be that ancient civilizations knew how to hack this effect? Could the carefully structured patterns in Hindu yantras, Islamic mosaics, and Gothic cathedrals actually be designed to shift human perception? If so, then geometry is not just a mathematical tool. It is a form of power. And those who knew how to use it—the architects, the scholars, the rulers of past civilizations—were not just builders. They were something else. Something more.

And now, that knowledge is almost gone. But why? And more importantly—*who still uses it today?* Its a question if we truly analyse then probably we are going to be successful in most of the fields of our life .

Cathedrals and Quantum Equations Speak the Same Language

I have never walked through the colossal halls of Notre-Dame or stood beneath the shadow of Chartres Cathedral, but I have seen them in movies and pictures,seen their towering spires, their stained glass fractals that catch the light like frozen echoes of something ancient. I have traced their floor plans with my eyes and paper, their impossible symmetry, their way of bending space and time without ever moving.

And then, one day, I saw an equation. It wasn't just any equation. It was something deeper—something eerily familiar. The Schrödinger wave equation while preparing for my exams . The formula that describes the fundamental dance of particles, the way reality itself ripples like stained glass catching the morning sun.That's when it hit me.

The Gothic Whisper—A Blueprint of Reality?

Gothic cathedrals were not just places of worship. They were machines, coded with mathematical precision. Their ribbed vaults, their pointed arches—they weren't designed just for beauty. They were constructed to amplify resonance. Step inside, and the space swallows you whole. The chants of monks once vibrated through these halls at precise frequencies, bouncing off the geometry in ways that could alter human perception. Sound waves. Light waves. Brain waves.

And if you compare the fractal patterns of rose windows—those spiraling, hypnotic designs that seem to pull you into some divine void—you will find that they match something else. The equations that govern quantum fields.Coincidence? Or did the architects of the past intuitively understand something ?

Entanglement in Stone—What Lies Beneath the Cathedrals

Some say the blueprints of these cathedrals weren't just drawn by men. That their dimensions, their ratios, their celestial alignments came from older knowledge—knowledge that might have been lost in fire, in war, in silence.

Did you know that most of these cathedrals are built over ancient pagan sites? That the ley lines—those invisible veins of the Earth's energy—run beneath them? It is almost as if the builders weren't just raising stone but channeling something unseen.

The Gothic cathedrals of Europe and the Brihadeeswarar Temple in India, separated by centuries and continents, share an eerie similarity—their towering structures follow sacred geometry, their interiors hum with the same harmonic ratios. One dedicated to a single God, the other to the cosmic dance of Shiva. But both speaking in a language older than words.

And here's the strangest part.The higher you go in the study of physics, the deeper you dive into string theory, quantum superposition, and the shape of reality itself—the more it begins to resemble architecture. Spaces folding, resonances aligning, dimensions curling into unseen corners. It makes you wonder—were cathedrals, pyramids, temples... not just structures, but equations written in stone? If so, then what were they trying to solve? And more importantly... who was meant to read them? And if we , you , me , the humans truly discover this essence or answer to this then we will evolve into something greater .

The Science of Sacred Shapes

Some patterns are universal. They transcend time, culture, and discipline—appearing in ancient religious symbols, biological structures, and modern physics. These shapes aren't just aesthetically pleasing; they follow mathematical principles that dictate the very essence of reality. But why do these shapes keep showing up? And more importantly—what do they reveal?

The Flower of Life – The Blueprint of Existence

One of the most mysterious symbols in history, the Flower of Life is a geometric pattern composed of multiple evenly spaced, overlapping circles. This shape has been found in: Ancient Egyptian temples, carved into walls as if carrying a secret message from a lost civilization.The Forbidden City in China, hidden within imperial designs. Leonardo da Vinci's notebooks, where he explored its mathematical and artistic significance.

Modern science now suggests this pattern mirrors the very structure of reality. Inside its geometry lies the framework for metatron's cube, the Platonic solids, and even the structure of DNA itself. Some scientists argue that its arrangement reflects how atomic structures and quantum fields interact, a concept strangely close to what ancient civilizations seemed to understand without microscopes or equations.

The Vesica Piscis – The Gate Between Dimensions

Imagine two circles overlapping, forming an almond-shaped space in the middle. This simple yet profound shape, known as the Vesica Piscis, has been revered across multiple civilizations: Early Christian art used it as the foundation of sacred symbols. Hindu and Buddhist yantras incorporated its form in spiritual diagrams.

Medieval architects used it in cathedral designs, believing it held mystical proportions.

What's fascinating is that modern physics has stumbled upon something similar. The Vesica Piscis resembles the patterns seen in wave interference and quantum entanglement. Some physicists even suggest that this shape may represent the way different dimensions interact, as if ancient knowledge hinted at truths we are only now beginning to grasp or perhaps remember .

I was reading the project review by Janice-Emmot on Vesica Pisis and that really challenged different ways of thinking . I would like to mention this part from her project - "*View yourself in the centre of the flower of life hologram, and allow the surrounding geometry to be the perfected form of our Auric or Buddha field. This allows access to your divine blueprint and wakes up the diseased organs to remember their Original Form; that is why Sacred Geometry is about remembering who you truly are." Jain 108, 2019*

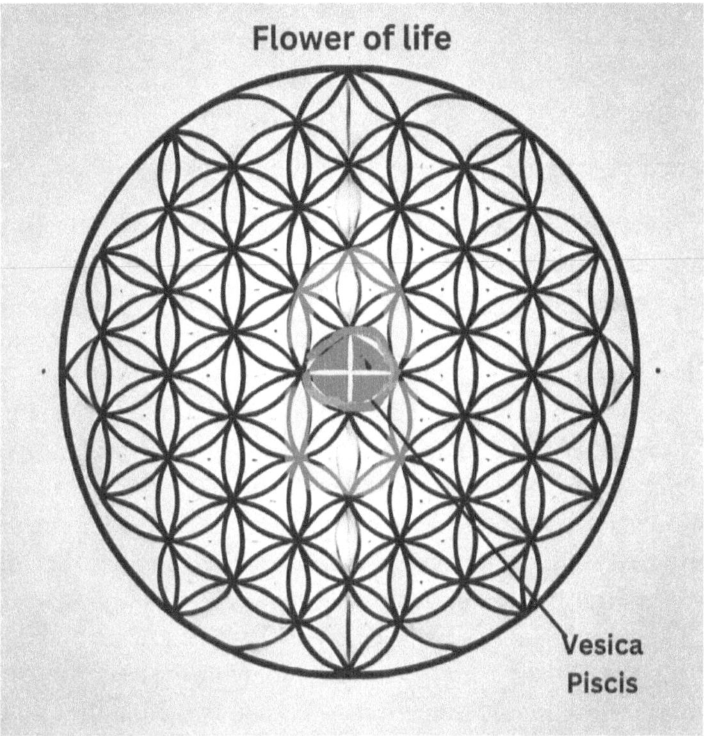

Flower of life and Vesica Piscis

The Platonic Solids – The Secret Code of Reality

Over 2,000 years ago, the philosopher Plato described five perfect three-dimensional forms—now called the Platonic solids. Each of these solids (tetrahedron, hexahedron, octahedron, dodecahedron, and icosahedron) holds remarkable properties: They appear in natural crystal formations.They dictate molecular structures in biology. They are used in quantum field models and energy flow systems.

But one of these shapes, the dodecahedron, was especially intriguing. In ancient times, it was considered sacred, representing the ‘ether’ or the fifth element, something beyond the physical world.For centuries, scientists dismissed this idea. In Timaeus, Plato described the dodecahedron as the shape of the universe because of its unique symmetry and connection to cosmic harmony. With 12 pentagonal faces, it mirrors the golden ratio, symbolizing balance and perfection. The dodecahedron closely resembles a sphere, making it ideal to represent the infinite yet enclosed nature of the cosmos. Its link to the 12 zodiac signs and mystical dimensions further deepens its symbolism as the blueprint of reality , a shape that bridges science, art, and the divine. Then in 2003, researchers studying the shape of the universe itself found something shocking. Data from the cosmic microwave background, the oldest light in the universe, suggested that space might not be infinite, but instead shaped like a dodecahedron.

In other words, Plato’s mystical intuition about the universe’s shape may have been right all along.These shapes are not just mathematical curiosities. They are the foundation of how nature builds itself. From the spirals of galaxies to the double helix of DNA, from the structure of ancient temples to the neural pathways in your brain, everything follows these hidden codes.

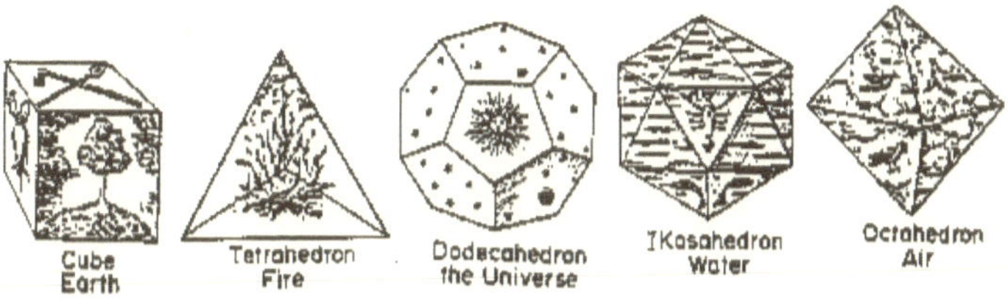

Platonic Solids

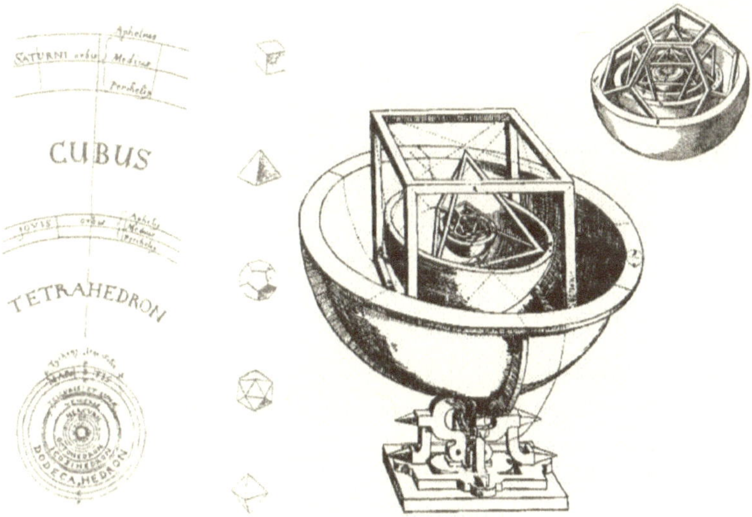

From Mysterium Cosmographicum by Johannes Kepler (1596)

But if this knowledge was so fundamental, why was it hidden?

Why Your Body Follows the Code

The human body is not just a biological machine—it is a masterpiece of geometry. Every cell, organ, and function follows mathematical precision, as if nature itself was an architect designing us according to a hidden blueprint.

The Fibonacci Sequence in Your Body

The Fibonacci sequence—1, 1, 2, 3, 5, 8, 13...—is a mathematical pattern where each number is the sum of the two before it. It's found everywhere in nature—spirals in sunflowers, branching in trees, even in the shape of hurricanes and galaxies.But what's even stranger? Your body follows the same pattern.Your fingers: Each section of your fingers follows the Fibonacci ratio.Your arm bones: The ratio between your forearm and hand aligns with the Fibonacci sequence.Your face: The proportions of your nose, eyes, and mouth all map onto Fibonacci ratios.Even the way your DNA coils into a double helix matches the Fibonacci sequence,as if the fundamental structure of life itself is following an ancient mathematical rule.

The Golden Ratio in Human Beauty and Biology

Closely related to the Fibonacci sequence is the Golden Ratio (1.618), also known as Phi. Artists and architects have used this ratio for centuries, believing it creates perfect harmony. But modern science shows your body is literally built upon it.Your DNA spirals in the Golden Ratio. Your heart's electrical system follows Phi in its rhythm. The proportions of your face, if considered "aesthetically perfect," align with Phi.

Even in medical science, Phi appears in the branching of your blood vessels, the shape of your lungs, and even in the proportions of the human brain. It seems as if life itself is following a divine mathematical law. which is also observed in art

.

The Mystery of the Dodecahedron and Your Brain

We talked about the dodecahedron in the last subchapter , the mystical shape once thought to represent the "ether" or cosmic energy. But what if I told you this shape appears inside your brain? Recent studies in neuroscience show that the neurons in your brain form interconnecting networks that resemble the dodecahedron. This isn't just a coincidence,it suggests that consciousness itself may follow hidden geometrical rules.

Some researchers speculate that your brain may use higher-dimensional geometry to process information, meaning that your thoughts, memories, and creativity might be linked to patterns beyond our three-dimensional understanding.

So What Does This All Mean? Your body is not random. Your DNA, your brain, your heartbeat—*everything follows a deeper code*, a universal pattern that connects you to the cosmos. If the ancient world knew this, if they built temples, art, and entire philosophies around these principles, then wonder what would happen if we find something that we haven't discovered yet.

The Fractals of Thought—How Your Mind is More Than Just a Machine

Close your eyes for a moment. Picture a tree, its branches spreading outward, each smaller limb splitting into even tinier branches, stretching toward the sky. Now, shift your focus inward—to the veins in your hand, the delicate network of neurons firing in your brain. Do you see the pattern?

Your thoughts are not linear. They do not flow in a straight, predictable path. Instead, they expand, branch out, and fold back onto themselves, much like the fractals seen in nature. But what if this wasn't just a coincidence? What if the very architecture of your mind was proof that your consciousness operates on a deeper, mathematical level ?

The Fractal Geometry of the Brain

Neuroscientists have long believed that the brain functions like a complex electrical circuit, with neurons transmitting signals in a structured manner. But recent discoveries suggest something far more intriguing: neurons fire in fractal patterns.The folds of your cerebral cortex mimic the branching of lightning bolts, the tributaries of rivers, and even the cracks in parched earth.Your neural connections do not just form straight pathways,they follow recursive loops, self-similar to trees and snowflakes.The EEG (electroencephalogram) waves of your brain form fractal-like structures, mirroring patterns found in coastlines, galaxies, and DNA.

Dont you think this itself follows the same rules as the universe.

The Hidden Mathematics of Memory and Creativity

Ever wondered why inspiration strikes suddenly, like a lightning bolt? Why a single thought can lead to a chain reaction of ideas? This, too, follows fractal geometry. Memories are not stored in isolated compartments—they are interconnected, like the repeating branches of a fractal tree. One thought leads to another, then another, forming infinite pathways. Creative thinking is not a straight line—it loops, expands, and folds onto itself, much like a Mandelbrot set (a famous fractal in mathematics). Dreams, hallucinations, and déjà vu—all seem to emerge from fractal-like activity in the brain, as if your mind is attempting to explore a limitless, self-repeating pattern.

Could this explain why some of the greatest thinkers—Da Vinci, Ramanujan, Tesla—claimed that their ideas "came to them" fully formed, as if plucked from a hidden structure of reality?

Fractals in Perception—Are We Living in a Simulation?

If your thoughts follow fractal geometry, what does that say about reality itself? Your eyes detect patterns in nature effortlessly, because they are designed to recognize fractals. This is why we find trees, waves, and even human faces so visually satisfying.

You should study fractals because they are the hidden blueprint of reality.Your lungs, for example, follow a fractal branching pattern, maximizing oxygen exchange without needing lungs the size of a room. In finance, stock markets display self-similar fluctuations across different time scales, allowing traders to predict trends and minimize risks. Fractal geometry is also crucial in AI and image compression, helping recognize patterns and store high-quality visuals efficiently. Even galaxies align in fractal-like cosmic web structures, hinting at a deeper order in the universe, an idea Plato speculated with his dodecahedral universe theory.

The way you process time is fractal-like, memories do not flow in a straight line; they expand and shrink, loop, and repeat. Some physicists now believe that the universe itself is a fractal structure, if so, does that mean your consciousness is simply mirroring the grand design of existence?

Perhaps the mind is not just a machine. Perhaps it is something far greater,a fractal reflection of the universe itself.

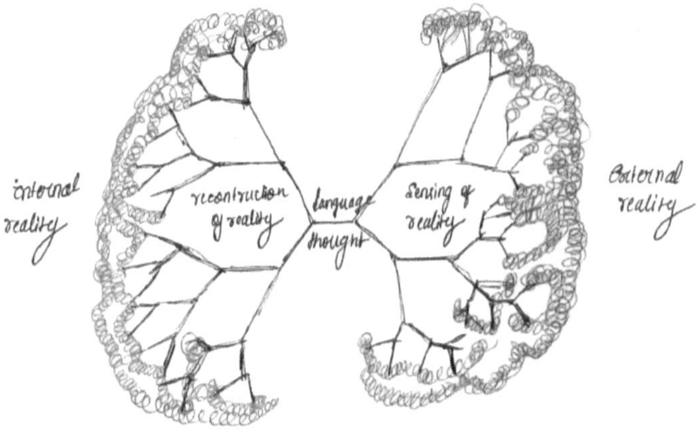

Fractals of Perception , Inspired by - Genetic Fractals

I was reading a blog by Genetic Fractals where the concept of fractals in human perception really caught my attention. The author explained how our senses and brains process the world through a fractal pattern. Our vision, for instance, works like a fractal. When we look at a scene, our brain doesn't process it all at once; it picks out broad shapes and colours first, then zooms in to break them down into even finer details. This process repeats endlessly, like the branches of a tree.

The fascinating part is that this fractal pattern applies to everything we perceive. The longer we focus on something, the deeper we can explore its details, just like peeling back layers in an infinite fractal. Our minds, in essence, are continuously scanning, simplifying, and breaking down the world into these repeating patterns, allowing us to focus on one small piece at a time while ignoring the overwhelming complexity of the whole. This idea helped me understand how our perception is limited yet infinitely detailed, shaped by a fractal process that lets us experience the world step by step.

Geometric Harmony: The Intersection of Art, Music, Dance, and Science

At first glance, science and art seem to belong to different worlds—one governed by logic, the other by emotion. But look deeper, and you'll see they share a common foundation: geometry. The same mathematical patterns that govern the stars, the honeycomb, and the human body also shape the most celebrated expressions of human creativity.

The Brushstrokes of Geometry—Painting and Symmetry

Artists have long used geometric precision to create harmony in their works. The Renaissance masters, from Leonardo da Vinci to Vermeer, relied on the golden ratios, vanishing points, and perspective grids to create paintings that felt alive. Even modern artists like Piet Mondrian used precise grids and primary colors to craft compositions that mirrored the ordered chaos of the universe.

But beyond aesthetics, geometry influences how we perceive paintings. The rule of thirds, used in both classical and digital art, mirrors the same spatial efficiency seen in nature,from the placement of leaves on a stem to the spiral patterns of galaxies.

The Sound of Symmetry—Music and Mathematics

Music, at its core, is structured mathematics in motion. The harmonic sequences in Beethoven's symphonies, the intricate ragas of Indian classical music, and even the pulsating beats of electronic music are all governed by geometric waveforms and frequency ratios.

Pythagoras' Scale and Sacred Geometry: The Greek mathematician Pythagoras discovered that the most pleasing musical notes correspond to simple whole-number ratios—creating what we now call harmonics. This same principle explains why the spacing of keys on a piano follows an exponential pattern and why octaves feel naturally connected.

Now the fractals in Music Composition, the recursive patterns found in Bach's fugues or Hindustani classical music's improvisations mirror the self-replicating beauty of fractals in nature,from fern leaves to the spirals in hurricanes.

The relationship between music and mathematical fractals is rooted in the idea that both follow patterns that repeat at different scales, revealing a hidden order that governs the universe. Researchers like Voss and Clarke uncovered that music adheres to a 1/f power law, a statistical phenomenon where the frequency of patterns decreases as the scale increases, much like the self-similarity found in fractals. This law shows that in music, the repetition of patterns at different levels, from the smallest notes to the overall structure of the composition, mirrors the fractal nature of the world.The concept of fractals in music extends beyond simple repetition; it speaks to the intricate, layered relationships within a piece. Hsu and Hsu's research on note intervals reveals that certain intervals and relationships between notes, across different musical genres, follow fractal-like patterns. These patterns are not just random or arbitrary but are rooted in an underlying mathematical structure that spans across the composition.

The Dance of Forms—Choreography and Physics

As a dancer, I know this — *movement is not chaos, but precision.* Geometry bends with each turn, physics pulses in every step. Dance is where geometry becomes kinetic—shapes set in motion, angles turning into rhythm. Classical ballet, Bharatanatyam, and even contemporary dance rely on precise angular movements, rotational symmetry, and spatial alignment to create visual harmony. In the physics of Pirouettes, a ballerina's pirouette follows the same principle as a spinning gyroscope,conserving angular momentum by pulling in their arms, just as a figure skater does.

But how dance is related with geometry ? The spiraling turns in Sufi whirling mimic the Fibonacci sequence, echoing the cosmic patterns seen in galaxies and shells. Symmetry, proportions, and spatial awareness are vital in choreography, ensuring balance and harmony on stage. While i was practicing the waltz that always facinates me ,i realised something .The arcs in a waltz mirror the curves of parabolas, while the sharp stances in classical forms like Odissi create triangular frameworks that symbolize stability and strength.

And to discuss the patterns in motion capture, modern AI and motion tracking have revealed that certain dance movements share mathematical ratios with natural animal motion, making human movement an extension of the natural world's geometry.Studies have shown that the arcs traced by a dancer's limbs often follow logarithmic spirals, similar to the way hawks spiral downward while hunting or the curve of a nautilus shell. Dancers instinctively create kinetic symmetry, balancing momentum and stability in patterns that mirror the fluid motion of fish in schools or birds in synchronized flight.

The Science Behind Creative Genius—Why It's All Connected

When we paint, compose, or dance, we are not just creating art; we are tapping into the same geometric truths that shape our universe. The fractal patterns in a Van Gogh painting, the wave harmonics in a Mozart symphony, and the fluidity of a contemporary dancer's movement all reflect the unseen architecture of reality.The genius of human creativity lies in its ability to translate these hidden structures into beauty—whether through a brushstroke, a melody, or a pirouette. And the closer we look, the more we realize:

The universe itself is an artist, and geometry is its masterpiece.

Unlocking the Unseen Forces

Throughout history, geometry has not only been a tool of logic and measurement but also a gateway to hidden forces—a secret key that civilizations have used to shape reality itself. From the towering pyramids of Giza to the intricate yantras of Eastern mysticism, from the harmonious chants of monks to the hypnotic rhythms of tribal dance, geometry has been more than a tool of beauty—it has been a force of creation, transformation, and influence.

The Power of Sacred Structures—Temples, Pyramids, and Mandalas

What do the Great Pyramids, Gothic cathedrals, and Hindu temples have in common? They are built upon strict geometric proportions that align with celestial forces.The Pyramids of Giza were designed with such precision that they align perfectly with Orion's Belt, hinting at an ancient understanding of cosmic geometry.The intricate carvings of Hindu temples, filled with golden ratios and fractal designs, were believed to harness divine energy, acting as "resonance chambers" that amplified spiritual vibrations.

Mandalas, used in Tibetan and Hindu traditions, represent microcosms of the universe, their swirling patterns guiding the mind into a state of meditation where deeper awareness is unlocked.Architects of ancient civilizations weren't merely building—they were tuning into an invisible blueprint of energy.And when i say blueprint ,imagine if we can have that ?

Cymatics—The Sound That Shapes Matter

In 1787, scientist Ernst Chladni discovered that sound waves could create geometric patterns in fine sand. When different frequencies played, the grains formed precise shapes—from hexagons to spirals. This field, known as Cymatics, proves that sound and vibration can physically manipulate matter.Ancient cultures instinctively knew this.Gregorian chants, Vedic mantras, and Sufi zikr all rely on repetitive vibrations, which are said to realign the body's energy field.Certain frequencies, like 432 Hz and 528 Hz, are believed to have healing properties, affecting the body's molecular structure.

Even modern music therapy relies on these principles, proving that sound can alter brainwaves and influence human emotions.While reading *The Man Who Mistook His Wife for a Hat* by *Oliver Sacks*, I discovered how patients with neurological disorders found unexpected clarity and calm through music. Similarly, in the documentary *Alive Inside*, I witnessed how music could awaken memories in those suffering from severe dementia, stirring emotions long thought to be lost. These moments reveal that sound isn't just an art form — it's science.

"By understanding the mathematics behind sound, resonance, and frequency, one can learn to manipulate reality itself."

The Body as a Geometric Vessel—Mudras, Yoga, and Gestural Energy

The human body is not just flesh and bone—it is a living geometric structure. The way we move, position, and align ourselves directly affects the flow of energy.Mudras (hand gestures) in Hinduism and Buddhism use precise finger positions to channel specific types of power.Yoga postures (asanas) align the spine with sacred geometric principles, activating energy centers known as chakras—which themselves follow a Fibonacci-like pattern in the body.

I remember when the mysterious man I mentioned in the acknowledgments once spoke to me about this. He wasn't like any teacher I'd known , his words carried a weight that lingered long after the conversation ended."Your fingers," he said one evening, "are not just limbs — they are keys." He guided me through a series of mudras , deliberate hand gestures, each finger bending and pressing with precision. At first, it felt awkward, almost meaningless. But as I held each pose, breathing deeply as he instructed, I began to sense something shift - not just in my body, but in my mind. There was focus, stillness, and an unfamiliar yet powerful sense of control.Yet his lessons didn't end with mudras. He spoke of something deeper —***"If you must live, live with rightful pride."***

Theoretically, mudras affect the nervous system by stimulating specific neural pathways, which can influence brain activity and mental states. This aligns with the concept of acupressure, where certain hand positions correspond to energy points within the body's meridian system. By activating these points, mudras are thought to improve the flow of energy , potentially enhancing physical and mental well-being.

Martial arts like Tai Chi and Kalaripayattu use circular and triangular movements to harness internal energy, allowing fighters to move with fluid efficiency.While practicing Taekwondo's jab punches (Jireugi) alongside the ancient martial art of Goddess Kali, I noticed a striking pattern ,both relied on geometry. In Taekwondo, Jireugi isn't just a punch; it's a straight-line force, driven by precision and alignment. In Kali's art, the strikes move like sharp triangles — swift, direct, yet fluid. One was disciplined and linear, the other instinctive and raw ,yet both followed the same silent rule, *angles create power.*You may find yourself wondering , how is it possible for one individual to immerse in such diverse pursuits: martial arts, dance, science, and art? But that's the thing , *everything is connected.*

To master one's body through geometry is to master energy itself.

You might wonder how one mind dances through science, art, and combat. The answer? *The boundaries between them are illusions.*

Art as a Portal—Activating the Mind's Hidden Powers

Every great artist, whether knowingly or unknowingly, taps into universal patterns that unlock the human mind's subconscious depths. The swirling, turbulent brushstrokes of Van Gogh's Starry Night match the mathematical equations of fluid dynamics, mirroring the motion of galaxies. The rhythmic dance of Kathak mirrors fractal motion, each movement is a repetition of a larger whole. The hypnotic designs in Islamic geometric art are meant to guide the viewer into a trance-like state, where deeper realities can be accessed.

Art is not just for expression, it is a tool for unlocking dormant abilities within the mind, a way to reshape perception, influence emotion, and even shift reality.

Final Thought—The Path to Mastery

If geometry, music, and movement have the power to shape energy, then to master these arts is to master influence itself. The greatest minds, the most powerful artists, the most advanced civilizations understood this—*geometry is not just a tool. It is a force.*

To those who see it, the universe is not just numbers and formulas—it is a symphony, waiting to be conducted.

CHAPTER FIVE

QUANTICAE

(Quantum Canvases: When Art Becomes a Multiverse)

"Where brushstrokes collapse possibilities and reality is but a stroke away."

Picasso & Einstein—Two men who shattered reality at the same time.

The world before the 20th century was simpler—stable, predictable, grounded in rules that everyone assumed were unshakable. Art followed perspective. Physics followed Newton. Time was constant. Space was rigid. Reality had structure.Then came Einstein and Picasso, two young men who saw the world differently—*who broke it.*

Einstein: The Man Who Warped Time

I first stumbled upon Einstein's ideas not in a classroom, but while reading 'Ideas and Opinions' — a collection of his essays that felt less like science and more like a conversation with a restless genius.In 1905, while working as a clerk in a Swiss patent office, Albert Einstein published a paper that rewrote the laws of the universe. His Special Theory of Relativity argued that-***Time is not absolute—it stretches and shrinks depending on speed.*** And this perfectly alligned with my theory which i wrote on my diary .

He also revealed that "*Space is not rigid, it bends under gravity's pull*". *Light moves at a fixed speed, no matter how fast the observer is moving*. This shattered everything people believed about reality. Imagine two people experiencing different versions of time, both correct in their own frame of reference. Imagine a beam of light ignoring the rules of motion. It was madness.

Now this made me do a comparision and basic understanding of this concept . Think of space not as a fixed, empty stage but as a living, flexible fabric that bends and moves based on what's inside it. Just like a heavy object creates a dent in a stretched-out sheet, everything we see and experience is shaped by the way space bends around massive objects. This means reality itself isn't absolute, it shifts depending on where we stand, how fast we move, and what surrounds us. *Even time flows differently depending on gravity's pull.* Now, if space and time can bend, stretch, and shift, it challenges the idea that our reality is fixed.

Just as massive objects bend space-time, powerful thoughts and actions shape reality. The stronger the force—whether *gravity or willpower—the greater the impact.* Visionaries, like massive stars, warp the world around them, pulling possibilities into orbit. If space isn't rigid, neither is reality, *we shape it by the strength of our presence and belief.*

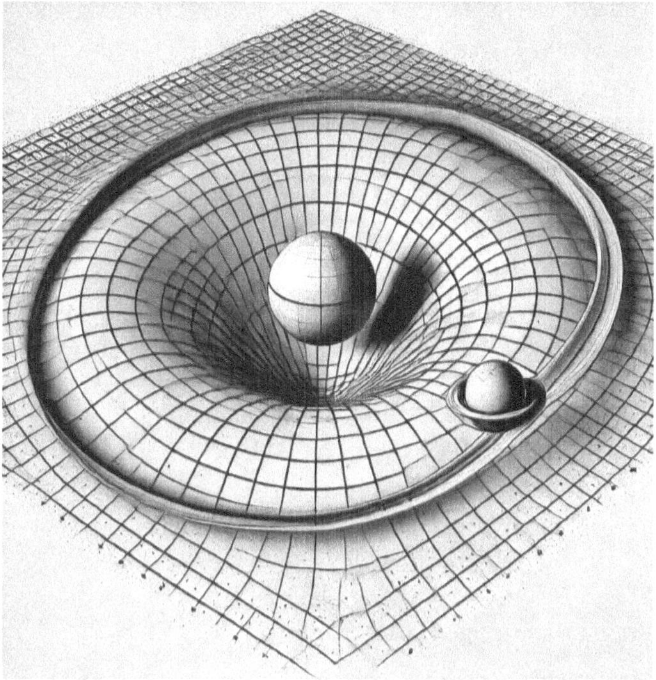

"Time and space are not conditions of existence, time and space is a model for thinking." - Einstein

Newtonian physics crumbled. Time and space, once seen as concrete, were now fluid, flexible, relative.And while Einstein was bending time in physics, Picasso was about to do the same to vision.

Picasso: The Man Who Fractured Vision

At the same time Einstein was reshaping the universe, a young Spanish painter named Pablo Picasso was about to rip apart the visual world. Before him, artists painted from a single viewpoint—what the eye naturally sees. Perspective and proportions ruled. But Picasso saw something else: What if a face could be seen from multiple angles at once?What if time, space, and motion could be compressed into a single frame? *What if reality itself wasn't fixed, but broken, like shattered glass?*

In 1907, Picasso painted *Les Demoiselles d'Avignon,* a chaotic masterpiece that marked the birth of Cubism. The women in the painting were not soft, graceful figures but fractured, angular distortions of reality. Their faces were sharp, some resembling African masks, others seeming to exist in multiple dimensions at once. People hated it. Art critics called it ugly. But Picasso had just done to vision what Einstein had done to time—he had proven that reality is not a single, fixed experience but a collection of perspectives, all existing at once.

A Strange Connection: Did They Know?

It's easy to think Einstein and Picasso were working in separate worlds,one in physics, the other in art. But history suggests otherwise. Picasso was obsessed with time and space, talking frequently with mathematicians and philosophers who debated the latest scientific ideas. Einstein, though deeply immersed in equations, was fascinated by perception and human experience—the way reality shifts depending on the observer.

And then there was *Poincaré*, the mathematician who unknowingly connected them both. Henri Poincaré was a physicist who influenced Einstein's ideas on relativity, but he also wrote about non-Euclidean geometry—*the idea that space itself could be curved and distorted.* These same ideas found their way into the conversations of Parisian artists, including Picasso's circle.

Did Picasso absorb the ideas of relativity before the world even understood them? Or was it something deeper—something woven into the very fabric of the early 1900s, pushing humans to break the illusion of a fixed, stable world? Whatever the answer, one thing is clear, *the moment Einstein and Picasso fractured reality, nothing could ever be the same again.*

The Art of Infinite Realities

Art is a paradox. The moment a brush touches canvas, a sculpture takes form, or a poem is inked onto paper, it ceases to belong to the artist. It fractures,splitting into a thousand interpretations, a thousand realities, each one valid. This isn't just poetic—it mirrors one of the strangest theories in *quantum physics: The Many-Worlds Interpretation (MWI).*

The Quantum Paradox of Observation

In quantum mechanics, an unobserved particle exists in a state of superposition- *meaning it is in multiple states at once.* It can be here, there, or anywhere, until someone observes it. The moment an observer interacts with it, the quantum wave function collapses into a single reality. But what if it never collapses?

The Many-Worlds Interpretation, proposed by physicist Hugh Everett in 1957, suggests that every possible outcome of a quantum event actually happens,but in separate, branching realities. Every decision, every moment of observation, spawns a parallel universe where an alternate version of reality plays out.*Now imagine this* , what if your life itself is a web of unseen branches? Each choice you didn't make, each path you overlooked , they might still exist, unfolding quietly in a reality just beyond your reach. The version of you who spoke up instead of staying silent, the version who turned left instead of right ,they are all out there, living stories you'll never witness yet somehow still belong to.

And what is art, if not a quantum event waiting for observation?

A Painting as a Multiverse

When you stand before a painting, what do you see? Some will find sorrow in its brushstrokes. Others will see passion. Some will see chaos, others harmony. And some will see nothing at all.

Each interpretation coexists, forming a network of possible meanings, much like quantum states. The moment you choose an interpretation, your reality collapses onto that meaning,but for another viewer, the painting is something entirely different. In this way, a great work of art functions like a quantum experiment. Each observer interacts with it differently, creating a web of realities where every interpretation is true, but only in its own universe.This idea has haunted artists for centuries.

Leonardo da Vinci's Mona Lisa—Is she smiling, or is it a trick of the eye? Her expression shifts depending on who looks at her, existing in multiple states at once. Turner's seascapes—Are they violent storms or peaceful oceans? It depends not just on the viewer's mind but also on their memories, emotions, and past experiences. Francis Bacon's distorted figures—Are they nightmarish visions or raw expressions of human fragility? Both. Neither. It depends on who is looking.

The artist might have painted with one intent, but the moment their work meets the world, it fractures into infinite meanings,each one a separate timeline, each one real in the mind of the observer.

Does This Mean an Artist Creates Universes?

If a single artwork contains infinite interpretations, each one forming a separate reality in the mind of the viewer, then the artist is, in a way, a creator of worlds. Strangely familiar to the physics we find boring in our textbooks ,isn't it ? Every brushstroke is a decision point. Every choice of color, shadow, or composition branches reality into different possibilities. Every observer, by engaging with the artwork, collapses their own version of the truth.

If Hugh Everett's Many-Worlds Interpretation is true, then every artist is unknowingly splitting reality with each creation. Their work does not exist in just one state but in all possible interpretations at once,until someone looks, and a single meaning solidifies, if only for a moment.

But if reality is just a shifting web of perspectives, can we ever claim to see the full picture? Or are we forever trapped in one sliver of a much larger, unknowable truth?

Schrödinger's Canvas—Exist here and there?

While researching quantum theories one afternoon with the company of sunrays reflected on my desk , I stumbled upon Schrödinger's paradox ,a cat that's both dead and alive until observed. At first, it seemed like an abstract puzzle. If a cat can be both dead and alive inside a box, can a painting be both masterpiece and failure at the same time? A cat is placed inside a box with a radioactive atom, a Geiger counter, and a vial of poison. If the atom decays, the poison is released, killing the cat; if not, the cat lives. According to quantum mechanics, until observed, the atom exists in both decayed and undecayed states simultaneously, meaning the cat is both alive and dead at the same time. This paradox highlights how observation affects reality at the quantum level, challenging our classical understanding of how things exist. Only when observed does it "choose" a single reality.

Now, let's apply this to art. A painting, unfinished and unseen in an artist's studio, exists in a state of uncertainty. Is it profound or meaningless? A stroke of genius or a mistake? A masterpiece or an abandoned mess? The moment someone lays eyes on it, the probabilities collapse, and a single interpretation emerges, but only for that observer. Someone else might see something entirely different.

This raises a haunting question,*does art even exist before it is perceived?*

The Forgotten Paintings That Became Masterpieces—Only After Observation

Some of the greatest works of art were once dismissed, abandoned, or forgotten—locked away in their own "quantum box," waiting for the right observer to open them.

{Van Gogh's Starry Night—A Painting That Almost Didn't Exist}

Van Gogh painted Starry Night while confined in an asylum. He thought it was a failure. His brushstrokes were frantic, his colors surreal. He wrote to his brother that the painting didn't work—he feared he had lost his artistic touch. It was ignored for years until the art world rediscovered it. Now, it is one of the most celebrated paintings in history.

Did Starry Night exist as a masterpiece before it was seen as one? Or was it Schrödinger's painting,both success and failure until the world chose?

{The Vermeer That Was Almost Lost}

The Girl with a Pearl Earring was forgotten for two centuries. Vermeer died in obscurity, and his works were dismissed. The painting sat in an attic, unnoticed. It was only in the 19th century that an art critic "opened the box" and declared it a masterpiece. Today, it is called the Mona Lisa of the North,but for 200 years, it was simply nothing.

Did it truly exist as a masterpiece until the right eyes saw it?

{The Hidden Sketches of Leonardo da Vinci}

Da Vinci's anatomical drawings were ignored for centuries. No one recognized their brilliance because they were too ahead of their time. Today, they are considered scientific treasures—proof that Da Vinci understood human biology centuries before modern science.

For 300 years, they weren't just paper ,they were waiting for an observer to collapse their reality into importance.

A Canvas That Chooses Its Own State

If paintings can exist in a dual state of value and worthlessness, does that mean a painting can change reality simply by being seen?

The Salvator Mundi, a painting attributed to Da Vinci, was sold in 1958 for $60—a forgotten relic. Decades later, it was declared authentic and sold for $450 million, making it the most expensive painting ever sold. Same painting. Same brushstrokes. Same canvas. Yet at one moment, it was worth nothing. The next, it was priceless. What is this ? Perhaps the painting changing itself or the the observation shaping the reality .

The Observer as the Artist—Do You Create the Art?

If every painting exists in superposition until it is seen, then the artist is not the only creator. If you see sorrow in a painting, did the artist put it there, or did you? If a painting makes you feel haunted, was it painted that way, or did your mind project that emotion into it? If a canvas remains unseen, does it even exist as art at all?

This is the paradox of Schrödinger's Canvas-*Art is both everything and nothing,until someone sees it.*And maybe, just maybe, the act of looking is the final stroke of every masterpiece.

The Power of Lost Art—What Can We Do With This Knowledge?

> “*"The great mystery is not that we should have been thrown down here at random between the profusion of matter and that of the stars, but that from our very nature we should draw images capable of denying our nothingness." (André Malraux's The Voices of Silence)*”

If lost art still exists in memory, then memory itself is a medium.We have been conditioned to think that art is only what can be seen, touched, or placed in a museum. But what if the true power of art lies not in its existence, but in its ability to transform minds—even after it is gone? If memory can preserve a painting, it can also create one .

Reconstructing the Invisible—How Memory Shapes Reality

Bringing Back the Lost

Historians have recreated lost artworks using AI, descriptions, and scattered sketches. Leonardo da Vinci's Leda and the Swan has been reconstructed by scholars, piece by piece—a painting reborn through thought alone. Does this mean that a painting doesn't need its original canvas to exist? Traditionally, we think of a painting as bound to its canvas. Once the canvas is destroyed, we assume the artwork is lost forever. However, if we can reconstruct it from memory, research, and digital technology, does it still count as the same painting? Or is it a new creation inspired by the lost one?

This concept challenges our perception of authenticity. If an artwork is only defined by the artist's brushstrokes, then reconstructions are mere imitations. But if art is about ideas, emotions, and expression, then perhaps a lost painting can be reborn even without its original medium. It suggests that art exists not just in physical form but also in collective consciousness, shaped by those who remember and reinterpret it.

The Mandela Effect of Art—Can We Remember Something That Never Was?

Some lost paintings are remembered differently by different people. Details like colors, figures, or entire compositions may be reconstructed based on personal perception rather than historical accuracy. Over time, the painting in our minds might become something entirely different from what originally existed. This leads to a fascinating possibility: Can an artwork be "created" by memory alone? If enough people believe in a non-existent painting and describe it with conviction, does that imagined artwork gain a form of existence? This raises questions about the power of collective belief and whether art is a product of reality or simply a reflection of human perception.

Art as a Weapon—The Power of Imagery to Control Thought

If paintings can live in the mind, who decides what is remembered? Throughout history, art has been a tool of influence—propaganda posters, religious icons, and national symbols have shaped entire societies. Governments, rulers, and institutions have used imagery to control narratives. But what happens when art is rewritten or erased? Lost artworks may not just disappear, they can be intentionally replaced with new versions that serve a different purpose.

For example, Propaganda replaces historical truth – Statues and paintings of leaders are altered or destroyed to change how history is perceived.Religious or ideological shifts – Sacred imagery is modified, censored, or erased to align with new doctrines.Cultural erasure – Colonizers, regimes, or revolutions have often destroyed or rewritten artistic traditions to reshape identity.If lost art is reconstructed inaccurately, it changes history itself. This makes art not just a visual medium but a battleground of ideas, one where control over images means control over thought.

How This Knowledge Applies to Reality

{The Future of Art Creation—Can We Paint With Thought?}

If an image can survive without existing physically, what stops us from creating art without paint? AI is now producing artworks based on human thought patterns. Scientists are working on technology that can generate images directly from brainwaves.

> “*"The day may come when artists will no longer use brushes or chisels to create masterpieces — they will simply think, and images will appear on a screen." (From The Future of the Mind by Michio Kaku)*”

And perhaps, one day, you or me can think of a masterpiece into existence.

{The Science of Memory—Can We Use Art to Hack the Brain?}

What if memory is not just a tool for preserving art, but for shaping the mind itself? Studies show that viewing certain paintings can alter neural pathways, triggering creativity and problem-solving. Some forms of therapy use visual memory to heal trauma, proving that even imaginary art can have real effects.

If we could control what images linger in our minds, then certainly we can reprogram ourselves .

{The Hidden Influence—How the Art You Don't See Still Controls You}

Even if you have never seen a missing painting, it may have shaped the world you live in. Entire architectural styles were inspired by lost artworks. Political movements have been driven by destroyed imagery,burned books, banned paintings, erased history. If lost art still influences the present, then does anything ever truly disappear? I dont think so.

Final Thought—The Mind as the Last Gallery

We exist in a world where reality is dictated by what we remember and what we forget. But if memory itself can preserve and create , then art, thought, and history are not fixed. They are fluid. They can be reshaped. *"And if we control what we remember, we control what is real."*

CHAPTER SIX

CHROMATICA

(The Hidden Laws of Colors & Shadows)

"Where light whispers secrets and darkness frames the truth."

What Your Eyes Refuse to See

> *"As sparks arise from a blazing fire, so from the depths of the imperishable, manifold beings are born and return to it again. The mind, deluded by illusion (Māyā), sees multiplicity where there is only One." — Mundaka Upanishad (2.1.1)*

Light is a liar. It shows us only what it wants us to see, draping the world in an illusion of clarity. But in truth, every color we witness is only a fraction of what exists,*what remains unseen is where power lies.* And those who understood the hidden nature of colors, who bent light to their will, have left their mark across time itself.

The Chemistry of Colors—Why Egyptian Blue Still Radiates After 4,000 Years

They painted with eternity in mind. The artisans of ancient Egypt, their hands dusted with crushed lapis and copper compounds, created something the world had never seen—Egyptian Blue, the first synthetic pigment in history. A color that does not fade, does not weaken, does not die. Even now, four millennia later, it glows beneath infrared light, whispering secrets through the centuries. Why? Because Egyptian Blue is not just a pigment. It is a key to energy itself.

The Science Behind the Glow

Egyptian Blue, or cuprorivaite, is woven with copper silicate, which gives it an ability no ordinary color possesses,it absorbs visible light and then re-emits it in the infrared spectrum. This means that even in complete darkness, it still radiates energy. Modern scientists have discovered its use in biomedical imaging and nanotechnology—a 4,000-year-old pigment now influencing future technology.

If color can store and emit energy, what else could it be used for?

The Power Hidden in Paint

The Egyptians painted their gods in blue, believing it connected them to the divine. But was this just belief—or knowledge? Infrared-sensitive pigments like Egyptian Blue could have been used in rituals that played with light beyond human vision. Imagine standing before a temple painting,one moment, a simple wall of color, the next, a luminous glow that seemed alive.Was this an early form of optical illusion? Not certainly, perhaps it the method to manipulate perception, to control what was seen and what was unseen.

The Vanishing Colors of the Ancients

Egyptian Blue survived. Others did not.Some colors once known to the world have disappeared without explanation .Maya Blue,a sacred color that refused to fade, yet its true method of creation was lost for centuries. Tyrian Purple,once worth more than gold, made from thousands of crushed sea snails, now extinct in its original form. Han Purple,used in the Terracotta Army, found to create quantum states of matter at extremely low temperatures.

These were not just colors. They were tools, codes, perhaps even weapons. And their disappearance begs a question—did they vanish naturally, or were they hidden?

What Your Eyes Refuse to See

Shadows hold just as much power as light. The optical tricks of Renaissance painters, who bent light with oil glazes to create illusions. "Ya Devi Sarvabhuteshu Chaya Rupena Samsthita" (The

Goddess who resides in all beings as shadow...) — Devi Suktam.

The invisible inks of spies, disappearing under normal sight but glowing under heat or ultraviolet rays.The natural fluorescence in butterfly wings, fish scales, even human tears—colors we are blind to unless the right light reveals them. So, what else have we failed to see? What else has been painted into our world, waiting for the right eye to uncover it?

The Alchemy of Shadows—How Darkness Shapes the World

> "*"The shadow is not merely the absence of light, but the keeper of unseen truths — where power gathers in silence, waiting to reveal itself."*
> *— Inspired by Eastern mysticism and Hermetic philosophy*"

If light reveals, then darkness commands.The human eye is a prisoner,enslaved to light, bound to its narrow spectrum, believing only in what it can perceive. But true power has never been in what is seen; it has always lurked in the unseen, in the shadows that stretch long and deep across history, in the ink that fades yet whispers through time.

Light lives on borrowed brilliance. It must exist in the presence of another, be it the sun, a flame, or the cold hum of electricity. But darkness? Darkness needs no permission. It is eternal, sovereign, untouched. Even in death, when light leaves the body, it is shadow that claims the bones.

But what if I told you that darkness is not the absence of light,it is a force of its own, a law in itself, shaping everything from art to war, from color to perception, from the birth of civilization to the conquest of empires.

Come, let me show you what the world has chosen to forget.

The Shadow Laws of Creation

Before an artist lays paint upon the canvas, before a sculptor carves the first mark into stone, before a scientist deciphers the mysteries of the atom—there is shadow. A void. A moment where nothing exists but potential.

Leonardo da Vinci did not begin with color. He began with shadows. Sfumato, his mastery of blurred edges, of darkness bleeding into light, was not just a technique—it was a revelation. He understood that the world does not move in rigid lines but in the uncertainty of gradients, in the slow dance between what is visible and what is merely suggested.And he was not the first to wield shadow as a weapon of creation.

The Greeks sculpted their gods with deep-set eyes and hollows in the marble, knowing that shadows would give them the illusion of movement, of divinity.The Japanese understood "Notan," the perfect balance of light and dark, where a single brushstroke of ink could command an entire scroll. Caravaggio bled his paintings in darkness, forcing light to emerge from the void like a whispered secret, shaping entire emotions with shadow alone.

But shadow does not only create beauty. It dictates reality. It hides truths. It bends minds.

The Science of Hidden Light

If the world were truly bathed in darkness, how would we see? The answer lies not in our eyes, but in infrared, ultraviolet, and electromagnetic spectrums,lights we cannot see but that govern everything.

Egyptian priests knew this before modern physicists ever put it into equations. They laced their temples with minerals that responded to heat and sunlight, making hieroglyphs glow under the right conditions. Not for the ordinary eye, but for those who knew where to look.Today, we call it thermal imaging, luminescence, and bioluminescence.

As observed in marine biology studies and scientific research on bioluminescence, deep-sea creatures craft entire worlds in absolute darkness, their bodies glowing with bio-chemical energy.Fireflies communicate through patterns of light invisible to predators but clear as words to each other.Plants reflect infrared waves, unseen by human sight, but visible to the birds and insects that rely on them. So what does this mean? It means that reality is not what we think it is. It means that *light itself is an illusion*, a mere layer draped over deeper, hidden forces.

"But if light is a lie, then shadows must be the truth."

The War Between Light and Shadow—Deception, Espionage, and Hidden Knowledge

What do the greatest military minds, the most powerful rulers, and the most elusive secret societies have in common?They understood shadows.

Napoleon did not win his battles with numbers—he won them with deception. He would light massive fires at night on one end of the battlefield, making his army appear larger than it was, while his real forces moved unseen through the darkness. The Cambridge Five, the most infamous spy ring of the Cold War, did not need weapons—they wielded invisibility, hiding in plain sight, using false identities, coded messages, and the deliberate absence of information to shift the tides of war.

And what of the greatest secret ever kept—the hidden city beneath the Vatican, where manuscripts forbidden to the public lie untouched, written in inks that only reveal themselves under the right conditions? Da Vinci's notes were written in mirror script—visible only in reflection, hidden from prying eyes. The Voynich Manuscript, a book written in an undeciphered code, remains unread to this day,was it written in a language of light, meant to be revealed under a spectrum we have yet to discover?

The CIA's Project MKUltra experimented with ways to control perception itself, playing with light, shadow, and suggestion to manipulate the human mind. Do you still think light is your ally? Or has it been a trick all along?

The Hidden Laws of Shadows in Everyday Life

You, too, are bound by shadows. Your brain interprets the world not as it is, but as it expects it to be.When you enter a dimly lit room, your eyes adjust, but your mind fills in the gaps you do not see, you assume.When you read a book, your brain does not register every letter; it anticipates the words before your eyes fully process them.When you dream, your subconscious uses shadows to form familiar shapes, morphing what is unknown into what is comforting or terrifying. Shadows influence you more than you realize. The way people stand in a room, the way an object is placed under a certain light, the way a simple shade of color can change your emotions , all of it is carefully designed, not accidental.

Advertising, propaganda, even architecture, all of them wield shadow as a psychological tool. Why are the halls of power built with towering columns, deep recesses, and long corridors of alternating light and darkness? Because your mind instinctively reacts to shadow with reverence, with fear, with submission.

The ancients knew this. The powerful still do. And now, so do you. So, what will you do with this knowledge? You could forget it, let it slip back into the void where it came from.Or you could use it.

*"Use shadows to see what others miss."*Use hidden light to uncover what was never meant to be found.Use the laws of darkness to command attention, to create, to control.Because those who understand both light and shadow are the ones who shape the world.

The rest? They simply live in it.

The Forbidden Colors—Shades That Were Never Meant to Be Seen.

Centuries ago, the great Arab philosopher and physician Ibn Sina (AD 980–1037), known in the West as Avicenna, explored the power of colors in healing. In his renowned work, The Canon of Medicine, he proposed that colors held remarkable influence over the body , red could improve blood quality, white could purify it, and yellow could ease pain and inflammation. He even warned against the use of red for those suffering from haemorrhoids, showing a rare understanding of color's complex effects.

Later, in 1876, the French scientist Augustus Pleasanton published Blue and Sunlight, claiming that blue light could not only relieve pain but also boost plant growth, increase fertility in animals, and even enhance physical development.

I came across these fascinating insights while reading *The Magic Therapy of Colours* by *A.R. Hari* — a reminder that the power of color is far more intricate than we often imagine.

What if I told you there are colors your eyes were never meant to witness? But beyond this thin veil of visible wavelengths, there are colors that defy our reality,shades that shimmer between dimensions, hues that once drove men to madness, pigments that have been buried, banned, erased from history.

Let me take you to the edge of perception. Let me show you the colors that were never meant to be seen.

The Colors That Shouldn't Exist—Impossible Hues

Our eyes obey strict laws. They perceive color through three types of cones—red, green, and blue. Every shade you have ever seen is a mixture of these three. But there are colors that break these laws. Imagine a red that is also green. A blue that is also yellow. You cannot, can you? And yet, they exist. These are forbidden colors, scientifically known as impossible hues. Under specific conditions—by tricking the brain, by manipulating the cones in your eyes—humans have perceived colors that should not be real.

I once read about an experiment that seemed too strange to be true ,something that made me write this chapter .In 1983, researchers Hewitt Crane and Thomas Piantanida conducted an experiment using retinal stabilization to prevent the eyes from separating opposing colors. The result? Subjects reported seeing a blue so deep it was darker than darkness, a red so intense it burned like an ember,yet neither shade could be described, only felt.

Some scientists believe that in rare moments—under hallucinogenic states, in near-death experiences, or within deep meditation—the brain bypasses its own filters, allowing people to perceive these hidden hues.If color is merely a trick of the brain, maybe we failing to see a lot things .

The Cursed Pigments—Colors That Were Erased from History

Some colors were never meant to be worn, never meant to be painted, never meant to last. Yet they were created—by accident, by greed, by genius. And then, one by one, they were erased.

Mummy Brown—A Pigment Made from the Dead

There was a time when painters sought a brown so rich, so warm, that it carried an almost supernatural depth. They found it in Egypt, in the bodies of the ancient dead. For centuries, European artists ground up mummified remains to create Mummy Brown, a pigment of haunting translucence. Its use was widespread until painters learned the truth. When the pre-Raphaelite artist Edward Burne-Jones discovered that he had unknowingly been using the dust of human remains in his work, he held a mock funeral for his paint tubes and swore never to touch the shade again. By the early 20th century, Mummy Brown had vanished. Or so they claim.

Han Purple—The Banned Color of the Emperor

Before China fell into its first great empire, alchemists created a pigment so unique that modern science struggles to replicate it. Han Purple was not just a color—it was a technological marvel, used to paint the warriors of the Terracotta Army and line the walls of the Emperor's palaces. But then, it disappeared.

No records explain why, but we now know this: Han Purple is not an ordinary pigment. It absorbs certain wavelengths of light and converts them into something beyond human vision—a property modern physicists associate with quantum mechanics. Some believe that the pigment held secrets of energy manipulation, leading to its suppression. Perhaps, some colors hold more than beauty. Perhaps, they hold power.

"*Research since its rediscovery has revealed remarkable properties of Han purple, including its ability to emit powerful rays of light in the near-infrared range and its capability to collapse three dimensions down to two under specific conditions.*" -(*Times of India*)

Vantablack—The Color That Devours Light

The blackest black ever created is not a color; it is an abyss. Vantablack, a material composed of carbon nanotubes, absorbs 99.96% of all light. It does not reflect, does not shimmer, does not bend—it swallows. A three-dimensional object painted in Vantablack appears two-dimensional, like a void cut into reality.

It is so potent that its use is restricted. No artist can legally obtain it. The British sculptor Anish Kapoor owns exclusive rights to the pigment, sparking controversy and leading to the creation of competing ultra-blacks like Black 3.0, which artists fought to reclaim.

But why was such a shade necessary? Perhaps you'll find the answer , if you dare to look closely enough. I did... and *what I found was more than just color.*

The Colors of the Gods—Biological Pigments That Shouldn't Exist

Nature does not create color. It only manipulates light. And sometimes, it does so in ways that should be impossible. Butterflies that are not blue. The wings of the Morpho butterfly shine in an ethereal, almost unnatural blue. But this is not pigment. The color is an illusion, created by microscopic structures that bend light. If you crushed the wings to dust, the blue would disappear,proving that sometimes, color is not something we see, but something we believe.

Birds that shift in the light. The feathers of the Nicobar pigeon shift between green, gold, and violet, but their pigment is dull. Their color is a trick—a masterful deception designed to make them appear otherworldly.

The Blood of the Horseshoe Crab. This creature has survived for over 450 million years, and its blood runs blue. Not metaphorically,truly, chemically blue, due to the presence of copper instead of iron. This blood is so valuable to science that a single liter can cost up to $60,000, and it is used to test for bacterial contamination in vaccines and medicines.What else in nature wears colors we do not yet understand?

The Lost Colors of the Future

If history has erased colors, then what colors have yet to be born? Scientists are already unlocking tetrachromacy, the rare ability in some humans to see 100 times more colors than the average person. These individuals possess a fourth cone in their eyes, allowing them to see shades no one else can even imagine.

What if we could engineer this ability? What new colors would appear before us? What if technology allowed us to paint in wavelengths outside human perception? What if there were colors beyond our spectrum,locked in the ultraviolet and infrared, waiting to be revealed? What happens when humanity stops being blind to the unseen? What Will You Do With This Knowledge?

This is not just a history of pigments. *This is a warning*. Color is more than a visual phenomenon,it is a tool, a weapon, a secret. Some colors have been erased from history for reasons unknown. Others have been locked away, hidden in vaults of science and art.

But what if those lost shades could return? Imagine painting in hues no one else can see , colors not just to be witnessed, but wielded. Power doesn't always reside in what's visible; sometimes, it is in what remains unseen.

The world belongs to those who master its hidden shades. *Now, that power is yours.*

A Madman Who Painted Fluid Dynamics Before Physics Could Define It.

Did he see the flow of the universe before anyone else?

The night swirls.A storm of blue and yellow twists across the sky, curling into spirals that seem alive, shifting, moving even when the paint is still. It is not just a painting. It is not just madness. It is an unintentional revelation, because hidden within Starry Night is a mystery that physicists spent centuries trying to define.

Van Gogh's Starry Night

Turbulence. A phenomenon so complex that even today, it defies complete mathematical explanation. And yet, Vincent van Gogh, in his fevered strokes, captured it with uncanny precision—long before scientists could even grasp the equations behind it.

But how?

The Secret Science in the Swirls

Turbulence is chaotic motion, the unpredictable flow of fluids,whether it's the way smoke curls from a candle, how rivers carve their way through rock, or how galaxies spiral across the void. It is one of the hardest problems in physics, one that Isaac Newton, Werner Heisenberg, and even modern supercomputers struggle to solve.

Yet in Starry Night, painted in 1889 while Van Gogh was in an asylum, the movement of the sky follows a mathematical pattern eerily close to the Kolmogorov scaling law, a theory of turbulence developed by Russian physicist Andrey Kolmogorov in 1941. The whorls and spirals in Van Gogh's sky match the eddies found in fluid turbulence. The gradients of color behave like the diffusion of gases in motion.The brightness variations in his paint follow a pattern similar to energy cascades in turbulent flow.

A 2004 study by physicists using digital analysis found that Van Gogh's paintings during his most mentally unstable periods—including Starry Night, Road with Cypress and Star, and Wheatfield with Crows—all contained mathematical turbulence, almost as if he had seen the hidden structure of fluid dynamics.

Was it madness? Genius? Or was he perceiving a deeper order in the universe, one the rest of us were blind to?

The Mind of a Visionary—Did Mental Illness Unlock Perception?

Vincent van Gogh was not just an artist. He was an enigma. A man whose mind existed on the edges of sanity, who saw the world in colors and shapes others could not comprehend. He wrote about hearing colors and seeing music. He painted light as something alive, radiating in waves rather than just illuminating a surface.His art became most mathematically precise when his mental state was at its worst.

Some neurologists believe that Van Gogh may have suffered from temporal lobe epilepsy, a condition that causes intense visual hallucinations. Others suggest bipolar disorder, which can heighten perception and cause a flood of creativity. But what if, instead of an illness, this was something else?

Some minds are simply tuned differently, like Tesla, who claimed he could visualize an entire invention in his mind before building it. Like Ramanujan, the mathematician who "received" formulas from a goddess in his dreams. Did Van Gogh, in his suffering, glimpse something no one else could? But to me,perhaps his madness allowed him to paint the physics of the universe before physicists even had the words for it.The world may label it as it pleases but an art that reveals the hidden science is truly a masterpiece and such a masterpiece deserves not just admiration, but respect.

The Unfinished Equation (Why Turbulence Remains a Mystery)

Imagine this , you're seated at a café in Paris, the air laced with the scent of roasted beans and rain saoked streets. You lift your cup, watching as a swirl of milk curls into your coffee , twisting, folding, unraveling itself in chaotic patterns. For a moment, it reminds you of something , a page you once read. Turbulence.

Even today, turbulence remains one of the most unsolved problems in science. It is the missing link in understanding how air moves over airplane wings, how blood flows through arteries, how weather systems form, how galaxies evolve.

Richard Feynman once called it "the most important unsolved problem of classical physics."

And yet, here was Van Gogh—alone, tormented, locked away, somehow painting its patterns without knowing the equations behind them. It raises a question more unsettling than any scientific mystery-Do we truly discover knowledge, or do some individuals simply remember what the universe has always known?

A New Perspective on Quantum Reality

In the same way that Van Gogh's paintings revealed swirling patterns that were eerily similar to the chaotic nature of turbulence, this theory postulates that the very fabric of reality what we experience as solid matter, energy, and time might itself be governed by fluid-like, turbulent dynamics. The mystery of turbulence that even the most advanced scientific minds have struggled to define might hold the key to understanding quantum mechanics at a deeper level.

This isn't just a wild metaphor . It's a serious call to rethink everything. Maybe particles aren't just waves or points in space , they're part of a flowing, shifting motion. A motion so complex, so alive, we're only just starting to glimpse its shape.

What Van Gogh may have witnessed, perhaps unknowingly, in his paintings could be a representation of this deep, universal turbulence that governs both the large and small scales of reality. His art might have captured a pattern of movement that corresponds not just to the visible world, but to the invisible undercurrents of the quantum realm, waiting for us to understand.

What This Means for You—The Artist as a Scientist

Vincent van Gogh's "madness" may have been more than just mental illness. It could have been a gateway to seeing the universe through a different lens, a lens that revealed the turbulent patterns beneath the surface of reality. Perhaps he saw what we are only beginning to theorize: that the universe, at its most fundamental level, is in constant, unpredictable motion.

As we continue to explore the quantum world, we may one day find that the turbulence Van Gogh captured in his paintings is not just a figment of artistic expression, but a deeper, universal truth—*a truth that bridges the realms of art and science, perception and reality.*

Van Gogh did not just paint. He revealed. He unlocked. He made the invisible visible. What patterns are waiting for you to see?

Turbulence at the Quantum Edge: Proposed by Theadra D.D.

The Turbulent Quantum Convergence Theory (TQCT)

While studying quantum mechanics, I came across a captivating NASA video that demonstrated the intricate patterns of turbulence in ocean currents and atmospheric systems. The video, showcasing data visualizations from NASA's Estimating the Circulation and Climate of the Ocean model, was a turning point in my research. As I watched the swirling motion of the currents, a striking realization hit me: Could the same principles of turbulence govern not only large-scale fluid systems, but also the quantum realm itself?

It is with careful contemplation and research that I propose a theory, which I shall call the *Turbulent Quantum Convergence Theory (TQCT).*

This theory suggests that the fundamental nature of reality ,across both macroscopic and quantum scales , is governed by turbulence: a dynamic, chaotic flow of energy and matter. Just as we witness turbulence in the swirling motion of ocean currents, weather systems, or the spiral arms of galaxies, I propose that everything from the behaviour of subatomic particles to the structure of space-time itself exists within a state of constant, unseen turbulence.

Now, I do not present this as an absolute truth. What I'm offering is not a final answer, but a possibility , one that has emerged through the course of my own exploration and study. It is a pattern I've started to trace, a thread that might just connect the smallest quantum events with the vast movements of the cosmos.

Introduction to Turbulence and Quantum Mechanics

Turbulence, as we understand it in classical physics, is the chaotic, unpredictable motion of fluids. This chaotic nature can be mathematically described by the Navier-Stokes equations,

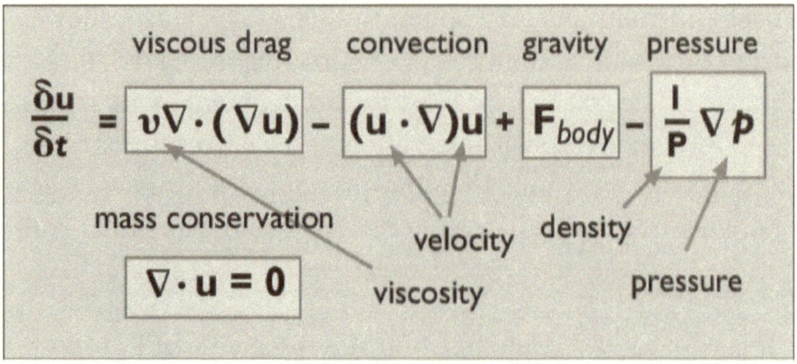

The Navier-Stokes equations for incompressible fluid flow

These equations, though powerful, do not have a general solution in turbulent flow cases, making turbulence one of the most complex and unresolved phenomena in classical physics.

Turbulence in Fluid Dynamics and Quantum Behavior

In classical turbulence, large fluid eddies break down into smaller ones, a phenomenon described by Kolmogorov's Scaling Law. This law explains the cascade of energy from large to small scales in a turbulent fluid:

$$E = v(\partial u / \partial x)^2$$

Where:

- ϵ is the energy dissipation rate,
- u is the velocity,
- v is the kinematic viscosity,
- x is the spatial coordinate.

The law shows how energy is transferred from large turbulent eddies to smaller, more chaotic eddies. If we extend this analogy to the quantum scale, we might speculate that the universe's fundamental quantum particles follow a similar cascade, perhaps existing in turbulence-like states at the quantum level.

Quantum Mechanics and Wave Behavior

Quantum mechanics is fundamentally governed by wave-particle duality, where particles exhibit both particle-like and wave-like behavior. The behavior of quantum systems is often described by the Schrödinger equation:

$$i\hbar \frac{\partial}{\partial t} \Psi(r,t) = \left[\frac{-\hbar^2}{2\mu} \nabla^2 + V(r,t) \right] \Psi(r,t)$$

$\Psi(r,t)$ is the wave function of the quantum particle, $\hbar$ is the reduced Planck's constant

This wave function describes the probabilistic nature of particles, an inherent uncertainty about their exact position and momentum, much like the chaotic, unpredictable nature of turbulence.

Fractals, Chaos Theory, and the Quantum Realm

At the core of turbulence is chaos theory, a mathematical framework that deals with systems sensitive to initial conditions, where small changes can lead to vastly different outcomes. Fractals, which are self-similar structures found at every scale, often model chaotic systems. Fractals are described by the equation,

$$f(z)=z^2+c$$

Where z is a complex number and c is a constant. Fractals are used to model irregular structures found in nature, such as coastlines, mountains, and even the distribution of galaxies. In a similar way, the fabric of space-time and quantum particles could be imagined as fractal-like, where turbulence exists at all scales, from the cosmic down to the quantum level.

Relating Turbulence to Quantum Systems

At the quantum level, particles are not stationary. They exist in a probabilistic wave state until they are observed. This inherent uncertainty and non-linearity echo the principles of classical turbulence, where fluid systems behave chaotically and unpredictably.

Heisenberg's Uncertainty Principle, which states that we cannot precisely measure both position and momentum at the same time, can be seen as a manifestation of quantum-level turbulence. This is mathematically represented as,

ΔxΔp ≥ ħ/2

This uncertainty comes from the chaotic, dynamic nature of quantum particles, which behave as though they are constantly in motion, just like fluids in a turbulent flow.

The Theory: Turbulence at the Quantum Level

Now, to connect these ideas, the Turbulent Quantum Convergence Theory (TQCT) proposes that the fundamental nature of quantum reality is not governed only by wave-particle duality or discrete particles. Instead, it can also possibly be driven by turbulence—*chaotic motion at the quantum level.*

This turbulence operates similarly to how we observe fluid dynamics at larger scales. In essence, quantum particles and fields could be seen as behaving like turbulent flows, constantly in motion, chaotic and unpredictable, yet governed by underlying patterns of energy and motion.

One can model this turbulence at the quantum level using principles from fluid dynamics. The idea is that as we zoom deeper into the quantum world, we might observe not just wave functions and particles, but a deeper turbulence, resembling the chaotic, ever-changing behavior seen in fluid turbulence. Mathematically, this could be represented as,

$$\Psi(\mathbf{r},t)=\int_{-\infty}^{\infty}A(\mathbf{r}')e^{-\frac{(\mathbf{r}-\mathbf{r}')^2}{2\sigma^2}}\cdot e^{i(k_x x+k_y y)}d\mathbf{r}'$$

(Quantum Turbulence Equation), acoording to my theory

Where,

- $A(r')$ represents a turbulent field interacting with quantum particles
- The exponential term suggests a wave-like interaction with a turbulent pattern,
- σ represents the turbulence scale of the energy cascade

As with Kolmogorov's turbulence model, we may propose that turbulence cascades from one quantum scale to the next, influencing how energy behaves and how particles emerge.

Conclusion: A New Lens to View Reality

In conclusion, The Turbulent Quantum Convergence Theory (TQCT) presents a radical idea, what if the universe, at every scale, from the macroscopic to the quantum—*is governed by turbulence*? Just as we see turbulence in the swirling ocean currents or the spiral of galaxies, we may find that turbulence is the fundamental property of the quantum world. This theory bridges the gap between the chaotic behavior of fluids and the strange, unpredictable behavior of quantum particles, suggesting that turbulence, not randomness, could be the driving force behind all physical phenomena.

But what could this mean for us?

It could change the way we understand not only physics, but consciousness, time, and even our place in the universe. If turbulence lies at the heart of all things, then perhaps our thoughts, emotions, and choices are also part of this grand flow interwoven with the same forces that move stars and atoms.

And maybe this explains why life often feels so complex—why human emotions can't be pinned down, why men and women often seem to be mysteries to each other, why relationships and the inner world defy clean logic. Maybe it's not because they are broken or irrational but because they follow the same laws of turbulence: intricate, layered, constantly moving beneath the surface.

If we begin to view life through the lens of this theory, we might start to see patterns where we once saw chaos, meaning where we once saw contradiction. TQCT doesn't just propose a new model for physics , it offers a new language for understanding reality, one that embraces complexity, motion, and the unseen rhythms that bind it all together.

By extending concepts from fluid dynamics, chaos theory, and quantum mechanics, we might begin to uncover a hidden structure in the universe, one that Van Gogh, in his swirling paintings, may have unknowingly captured or perhaps he was in a state of recieving very profound knowledge and we called it mental illness.

Your Eyes Lie to You Daily.

“*"Everything we see is but a shadow of what is." — Plato*”

Seeing is believing? Or is it deception? What if I told you that nothing you see is real.

Not in the way you think. The colors you adore, the objects you recognize, the depth you perceive, it’s all a carefully orchestrated illusion, a performance staged by your brain to make sense of a chaotic world. You trust your eyes, but they betray you every moment. The question is, why?

The Science of Deception—Why Your Brain Lies to You

Your eyes capture light, but they don’t see. Seeing happens in the brain, and your brain does not care about reality,it cares about efficiency.

Think of it as a lazy artist, filling in gaps rather than painting every detail. The brain has limited bandwidth, so it filters, guesses, and even fabricates visual information to create a world that feels seamless. It prefers speed over accuracy. This is why you can be fooled by an optical illusion-"*your mind is not showing you the truth, just its best guess.*"

Case Study: The Hollow Mask Illusion

If you look at the inside of a concave mask, your brain will force it to appear convex.Even when you know it’s an illusion, you can’t override your perception. Why? Because the brain has been conditioned to expect faces to be convex,it refuses to see otherwise.

This is not just a trick,it's proof that your brain prioritizes patterns over reality. It will bend the truth to fit what it expects.

The Hidden War—How Your Brain Edits Reality

Every second, your brain receives 11 million bits of sensory data, but your conscious mind can only process 50. The rest is discarded, edited, or altered. You do not experience the world as it is. You experience the world as your brain chooses to present it. This is why,

Imagine this , a beautiful girl stops you on the street, a dress draped over her arm. In the sunlight, it gleams white and gold ."Isn't it stunning?" she asks. You agree. But then she invites you inside her shop. Under the cold glow of artificial light, the dress turns blue and black. "It's always been blue and black," she says, laughing. But you're certain ,you saw white and gold.

That evening, curiosity gnawed at you. You couldn't shake the feeling — how could something so ordinary defy your senses? You searched for answers, and what you found unraveled something far greater than just a dress. There was the Café Wall illusion, where rows of perfectly parallel lines seemed to tilt and break. The brain, desperate for patterns, bent reality itself to make sense of it. Then came the Rotating Snakes illusion ,a still image that seemed to pulse and coil like something alive. There was no movement, yet your mind insisted it was there.

And that's when it struck you ,your eyes are not truth-tellers; they are negotiators. They don't show you the world as it is , they show you what your mind expects to see.Your brain has been sculpting an illusion your entire life. How much of what you think you see is even real?

The Ancient Deception—How Artists & Scientists Exploited Illusions

Throughout history, some individuals have understood and manipulated this flaw in human perception.Leonardo da Vinci used sfumato, a painting technique that blurred edges and tricked the eye into seeing depth that wasn't there. M.C. Escher created paradoxical structures that the brain could not reconcile.Greek sculptors designed statues with exaggerated proportions so they appeared perfect when viewed from below. Neurologists use illusions to map how vision and consciousness are constructed inside the brain. Even today, magicians, advertisers, and designers exploit these flaws to control what you see, and in turn, what you believe.

If you accept that your vision is but a carefully crafted illusion, a thing shaped rather than fixed, then you must ask yourself—who else holds the chisel? The merchant, who paints gold upon bronze and sells it as treasure. The ruler, who feeds illusions to the masses so that they remain blind to the truth. The scholar, who bends perception so that knowledge may be unearthed from deception.

Should you choose to wield this knowledge, you may become one of two things—a master of truth or a weaver of illusions. The choice is yours, reader.

> “*"Everything we hear is an opinion, not a fact. Everything we see is a perspective, not the truth." – Marcus Aurelius*”

CHAPTER SEVEN

MYSTICAE

(The Science of Mystical Art)

"When logic bends to beauty and symbols speak in equations."

Why do symbols haunt us?

"Bachofen said "Symbols guide the spirit, beyond the power of the finite state of becoming, into the realm of the infinite.""

Since the dawn of civilization, humans have been obsessed with symbols—etched into temple walls, hidden in paintings, embedded in the very foundation of alchemy and science. They speak a language older than words, a form of knowledge so primal it bypasses logic and strikes at something deeper-intuition.

But why? Why does a sigil make us uneasy? Why do ancient symbols persist across cultures that never met? Why do they seem to work, even when stripped of their mystical context? Because symbols are not just art. *They are a code*,one that holds the forgotten bridge between science and mysticism. Science and mysticism are two forces that, when united, unlock the deepest truths of the universe. One dissects the known, the other whispers the secrets of the unseen. Together, they transcend the limits of reason and intuition, revealing a reality far beyond our perception.

"Some of the greatest scientists were also mystics in disguise."

Alchemy—When Symbols Were Science

Before chemistry, before physics, before the microscope and the periodic table, there was alchemy-the oldest and most mysterious form of scientific pursuit. The alchemists did not separate science from art, nor from spirituality. To them, transformation was not just about substances but about the universe itself.

The pursuit of gold was never just about wealth. It was a symbol—the perfection of matter, the philosopher's stone that could transmute the base into the divine. They believed that nature had a secret language, and that language was made of symbols, numbers, and transformations.

And strangely enough,modern science proves they weren't entirely wrong.

The Hidden Chemistry of Gold—Did the Alchemists Almost Succeed?

For centuries, alchemists believed gold could be created through secret processes. Modern nuclear physics shows that, in a way, they were onto something.Gold can be made. Just not the way they thought. In particle accelerators, base metals can be transmuted into gold,proving that matter is not fixed, but fluid under the right conditions.

Stars themselves create gold in the heat of their dying explosions -alchemy, written into the cosmos itself.Ancient Chinese alchemists, obsessed with the elixir of life, mixed mercury and sulfur to try and make cinnabar, accidentally discovering early chemical reactions still used today.

Alchemy was not a failure. It was simply science without proof—a discipline centuries ahead of its time.

The Power of Sacred Symbols—Why Do They Feel Alive?

Some symbols linger, passing through history untouched, unforgotten. The Eye of Horus, an ancient symbol found within the sacred chambers of Egyptian tombs, resonates deeply with the very proportions of the human pineal gland ,a curious connection between mysticism and neuroscience. The Ouroboros, the serpent eternally consuming its own tail, mirrors the endless cycle of life and death, echoing the self replicating nature of DNA itself. The Sri Yantra, a geometric design revered in Hindu tradition, aligns with the intricate patterns found in modern fractal mathematics, an expression of the universe's infinitely recursive beauty. And the Golden Ratio, 1.618, not only appears in the petals of flowers and the spirals of seashells but is also observed in galaxies, the cosmos itself revealing a profound mathematical harmony between order and chaos.

These are not random. They reappear because they are woven into the fabric of reality itself. They are not mere decorations but visual formulas,hints at a deeper, universal truth.

How Artists Used Science to Hide Secrets in Plain Sight

Some of the greatest artists were also scientists, magicians of the mind who embedded symbols in their work, knowing that *some would see, and others would only sense.*

Leonardo da Vinci's paintings contain hidden geometry—his "Vitruvian Man" is an anatomical study, a mathematical code, and a mystical diagram in one. Salvador Dalí fused art with quantum mechanics, showing time as fluid before physics could explain it. Ancient cathedrals were designed using sacred geometry to induce a sense of awe and mystery,not by accident, but by architectural science. Symbols have power because they bypass logic. They communicate with the subconscious, activating something deeper,a knowledge older than language itself.

What This Means for You—Can You Read the Hidden Language?

If symbols persist across time and science confirms their strange effects, then perhaps we have been blind to an ancient truth

.There is a hidden structure to reality. It reveals itself in symbols. It whispers through art. It lingers in the laws of the universe itself. So you say , the one who is reading this , do you still see the illusion of separation ?

And those who learn to read it—
never see the world the same way again.

Symbols as Keys to Reality

I once read that the circle is a symbol of the psyche , even Plato described the soul as a sphere. The square, by contrast, binds itself to the earth , structured, rigid, a symbol of the body and reality. It struck me then, what happens when *the infinite mind is caged within the finite world?* Perhaps that's where symbols emerge , not just as shapes, but as keys. Do they hold some intrinsic energy, or are they psychological tools designed to unlock deeper layers of the mind?

To answer this, we must venture into neuroscience, quantum physics, and biology , because art and mysticism are not separate from science. They are merely the unexplained branches of it.

How Symbols Rewire the Brain—The Neuroscience of Sacred Imagery

Modern neuroscience suggests that symbols are not just learned but may be natural , hardwired into the brain itself. Carl Jung's theory of the collective unconscious suggests that certain symbols, archetypes, are embedded in human psychology from birth. The fusiform gyrus, the part of the brain responsible for facial recognition, is also activated by sacred symbols , as if the brain instinctively knows their meaning, even without prior exposure.

Studies on Tibetan monks show that meditating on mandalas (geometric spiritual diagrams) changes brain wave patterns, altering consciousness itself. This suggests that symbols do more than represent ideas , *they physically alter the mind.* Perhaps that is why a stranger can stand before an ancient emblem, one they have never seen, and feel as if they are being watched. Not by eyes, but by meaning itself , profound, silent, and undeniable.

Could this be why certain sigils, religious emblems, and ancient markings invoke feelings of awe, fear, or enlightenment? Are they activating something in us that logic alone cannot grasp?

Quantum Symbolism—Can an Image Change Reality?

If observation itself can alter reality , as proven by the famous double-slit experiment in quantum mechanics , then what happens when thousands, or even millions, of people focus on the same symbol?This is the basis of sigil magic, a concept ancient alchemists and even modern advertisers exploit.Logos of corporations function exactly like sigils—Nike's swoosh, Apple's bitten apple, McDonald's golden arches, simple symbols that trigger subconscious reactions.

Religious symbols have shaped entire civilizations, not just through belief but through physical effects on human behavior and history. Mass visualization experiments suggest that when large groups of people focus on a single image or intention, events in reality seem to shift, though science struggles to explain how.

Take for example *The Simpsons* , in one episode from the year 2000, Lisa Simpson becomes President and mentions inheriting the role from Donald Trump. Sixteen years later, Trump was elected as the 45th President of the United States. Another episode from 1998 showed 20th Century Fox as part of Disney,a deal that became real nearly two decades later. Coincidence? Maybe. But it's unsettling how often these fictional symbols have mirrored real events.

What if just by being in limelight of a larger mass this image or symbol did manifest itself ? What if symbols do not just communicate ideas but reshape the fabric of perception itself?

Biological Alchemy—Can Symbols Affect the Body?

Ancient cultures believed symbols could heal, transform, even extend life. Today, science is beginning to confirm some of these possibilities. The placebo effect, a sugar pill can heal the body if the patient believes it will, proving that the mind itself can trigger real physiological change. Cymatics,when sound frequencies vibrate on a metal plate covered in sand, they form perfect geometric patterns,suggesting that shape and sound are intrinsically linked. Pineal gland activation,some believe symbols like the Eye of Horus correspond directly to the structure of the brain's pineal gland, an organ linked to perception and possibly even altered states of consciousness.

Is it possible that the ancients knew how to use symbols as biological keys, *ways to activate hidden abilities within the body and mind?* And perhaps now is the time to ask yourself ,what knowledge have you forgetten.

What This Means—The True Power of Art, Science, and Symbols

Symbols are not just historical artifacts. They are living forces, shaping human thought, influencing physical matter, and possibly unlocking abilities we do not yet understand. If neuroscience proves symbols change the brain... if quantum physics hints that observation alters reality... if biology shows the mind can heal the body...

Then perhaps the line between art, science, and magic never existed at all. Those who understand this ,
those who learn to read the symbols , do not just see the world.
They reshape it.

The Forbidden Alphabet

What if I told you, reader, that symbols hold such power that writing them down is enough to awaken something? Throughout history, there have been whispers of lost alphabets , scripts so dangerous that entire civilizations erased them, terrified of what they might summon. But ideas do not die. They resurface , sometimes disguised, sometimes hidden in plain sight , waiting for someone curious enough to find them.

The Alphabet of the Gods—Scripts That Should Not Exist

Some languages were never meant for human tongues.

The *Enochian Language* – A supposed "angelic script" recorded by John Dee and Edward Kelley in the 16th century. They claimed it was the language of creation, used by angels to shape reality. Strangely, some linguists find its structure eerily mathematical, as if engineered, not invented. The *Voynich Manuscript* – A book filled with an undeciphered language, containing symbols no one can translate. Some believe it was not meant for humans, but for a mind more advanced—or for a species yet to come.The *Rongo-Rongo Script* – Found on Easter Island, this writing system has never been fully decoded. Was it erased on purpose?

If language is the tool we use to shape thought, then what happens when we speak words we were never meant to?

Cursed Words—When Speech Becomes a Spell

Some words should never be spoken aloud. Ancient cultures believed in the power of forbidden names, words that, when uttered, could bend reality.

The True Name of God , Jewish mysticism speaks of the Tetragrammaton (YHWH), a name so sacred it was never meant to be pronounced. Some say it is because the vibration of the word could alter existence itself. The Lost Word of the Freemasons , a secret word known only to the highest initiates, believed to hold the key to hidden knowledge. The "No-No Words" of Cultures , some African and Asian tribes forbid saying certain names aloud, fearing they will call forth spirits.

If sound carries energy, what happens when the wrong frequency is spoken into reality? Ask yourself, what sounds have you pronounced in your lifetime to shape the world around you.

Symbols That Do Not Belong Here

Some symbols have appeared throughout history, without explanation. The Flower of Life appears in temples, manuscripts, and ancient ruins across different civilizations that had no contact with each other. How did they all know this symbol? The Hand of the Mysteries, an ancient gesture found in hidden societies, appears in secretive paintings and manuscripts. Its meaning? Unknown. The Sator Square, a Latin palindrome that appears in medieval churches, Roman ruins, and even magic texts. Scholars cannot explain why it shows up everywhere.

“*"He who grasps the Hand of the Mysteries receives the keys to the hidden wisdom of all ages."*
— Manly P. Hall, The Secret Teachings of All Ages”

It is almost as if certain symbols are meant to be found, but not understood. Or maybe we are unable to .

The Unfinished Language—The Sentence That Ends the World

What if there is a sentence that, when completed, unlocks something hidden in reality? The Mayan Dresden Codex suggests a missing sequence of glyphs, some believe they foretold the end of an age. The Bible Code theory suggests secret messages hidden within sacred texts, but what if those messages are incomplete. The Antikythera Mechanism, an ancient computer, suggests that people once calculated the future, but its final settings are missing.

> “*"The Bible Code reveals a hidden text within the sacred scriptures — a code that seems to predict events long before they unfold, concealed in patterns only mathematics could unveil."*
> *— Michael Drosnin, The Bible Code*”

If there is a phrase that rewrites reality, perhaps it is unfinished for a reason. Perhaps, the universe is waiting for someone to complete it.

The Final Warning—Should We Keep Searching?

ASK YOURSELF . You know the answer for youself . Some knowledge was erased for a reason. Some scripts were forgotten, some names were banned, some symbols buried.

Was it ignorance that wiped them away? Or was it protection? The greatest minds in history have searched for the missing pieces,s ome vanished before they could share what they found.

If you learn the truth, what will you do with it?
And more importantly— Will it let you go?

The Art of Concealment—Knowledge Hidden in Plain Sight

Some truths are not lost. They are deliberately buried under layers of symbols, disguised as myths, encoded in paintings, and whispered in poetry. If you wish to hide something from the unworthy, where do you place it? In plain sight,where only those who know how to look will find it. Like now ,you are here , do you think its not put in plain sight ? Ofcourse it is , this is in midst of the mass but is this book in the hands of everyone ? No , only for the one who truly seeks.

The Paintings That Speak in Code

Some paintings do not just depict reality, they alter it. Hidden within brushstrokes, geometry, and perspective are messages that most will never see.

Da Vinci's Last Supper , the angles, hand gestures, and even the spacing of the apostles have been suspected to hold mathematical harmonies and hidden messages. Some claim the painting contains a secret piece of music, embedded within the positioning of hands and loaves of bread. But was it more than art? Some believe it was a coded map of celestial alignments, a visual manuscript for alchemical rituals , where beauty concealed a science few were meant to understand.

Van Eyck's Arnolfini Portrait ,a mirror in the background reveals figures unseen, implying that the viewer is being watched. The painting is signed with a cryptic Latin phrase, "Jan van Eyck was here." Was this a signature, or a warning?

> "*"Art does not reproduce the visible; rather, it makes visible."*
> *— Paul Klee, Creative Credo (1920)*"

Some art does not simply depict the world. It encodes knowledge about it.

Literature as a Cipher—Books That Whisper Secrets

Words are not merely ink on paper. They are codes, waiting to be deciphered. Some books are not meant to be read the way they appear. They are veiled in allegory, layered with double meanings, and disguised as mere fiction, yet they hold the weight of hidden knowledge , messages left behind for those who know where to look.

{Shakespeare—The Architect of Hidden Messages}

What if Shakespeare was not just a playwright, but a messenger? His works are woven with historical secrets, political warnings, and encrypted codes that some believe were placed deliberately. His sonnets contain numerical patterns that align with esoteric knowledge, and certain passages in his plays mirror the cryptic writings of occult philosophers of his time. Some even suspect that Shakespeare was not one man, but a collective, a façade for hidden scholars with a purpose greater than entertainment.

Take Shakespeare's First Folio, for example , a collection of 36 plays published in 1623. On the title page lies an odd engraving of Shakespeare, yet something feels... off. Scholars have noted that the collar sits unnaturally, almost as if it's drawn over an incomplete figure. The shadows on his face seem misaligned, as if two profiles have been merged. Some believe this is no accident , that it hints Shakespeare was merely a mask for someone else.

“*Then there’s Sonnet 14, where Shakespeare writes,*

"Not from the stars do I my judgment pluck,
And yet methinks I have astronomy."”

On the surface, he rejects astrology , yet deeper analysis reveals numerical patterns within the sonnet’s structure that align with star charts and planetary cycles. Some researchers argue this was a hidden nod to Hermetic traditions , suggesting Shakespeare was encoding cosmic knowledge into verse.

{Dante’s Divine Comedy—A Journey or a Map?}

On the surface, The Divine Comedy is a poetic odyssey through Hell, Purgatory, and Heaven. But is it just a story? Or does it conceal something greater? Some believe Dante’s descent through the Inferno is not simply a tale of the afterlife, but a coded guide to enlightenment, each circle of Hell representing stages of spiritual transformation. His descriptions of celestial alignments correspond to hidden astronomical knowledge, and his placement of historical figures suggests a deeper political message.

Dante’s celestial descriptions align curiously with known astronomical movements. His placement of stars, constellations, and planetary cycles has led some to believe The Divine Comedy encodes insights about cosmic order , a map not just of the soul’s journey, but of the universe itself.

{The Tao Te Ching—A Guide to Power Beyond the Physical}

A mere collection of poetic verses? Or a manual for reshaping reality? The Tao Te Ching, written by the elusive Laozi, appears to be simple wisdom on harmony and balance. But hidden within its verses are formulas that resonate with the principles of quantum physics, alchemy, and metaphysical energy manipulation. It speaks of the power of the void, of how the unseen governs the seen, a concept strangely similar to what modern science now understands about dark matter. Perhaps Laozi was not only just a philosopher but who had glimpsed the fabric of existence itself.

{The Voynich Manuscript—A Book That No One Can Read}

Then, there are books that refuse to reveal their secrets. The Voynich Manuscript, a centuries-old book written in an unknown language, filled with strange illustrations of celestial diagrams, medicinal herbs, and cryptic figures, remains undeciphered. Scholars, codebreakers, and even AI models have failed to translate it. Some believe it is an alchemical text, a lost codex of ancient knowledge, or even a book not meant for human understanding. But if it was written, then someone, somewhere, must have known its purpose.

These books do not merely contain stories. They are layers of knowledge, encoded and disguised, waiting for those with the eyes to see beyond the words. The question is—will you be among them?

Forbidden Frequencies of the Gods

In the beginning, there was sound.

The ancients whispered this truth in their temples, inscribed it on forgotten scrolls, and built their most sacred sites in harmony with it. They did not need equations to prove it, for they felt it in their bones, in the echo of their chants, in the rhythm of their footsteps against temple stone. They knew something we have forgotten: Sound is not just music. It is power.

The pyramids of Egypt were not built by mere hands. Or at least, not by hands alone.
The towering spires of Angkor Wat, the megaliths of Stonehenge, the whispering halls of the Parthenon—all of them were designed with one secret in mind: *resonance.*

Deep within the King's Chamber of the Great Pyramid, there is a room where sound does not merely echo—it lingers, vibrating against unseen walls, amplifying itself in ways no modern architect can fully explain. It is not an accident. *It is a key.* What if sound could lift stone? What if, instead of brute force, the ancients tuned into frequencies that made rock weightless?

Legends tell of monks who hummed stones into the sky, of builders who sang blocks into place. In the 1930s, a Swedish doctor named Henry Kjellson claimed to have seen Tibetan monks levitating massive boulders using sound alone. Their instruments,drums, trumpets, and their own voices,were arranged in a precise geometric pattern. He was ignored, of course. Dismissed.

But today, physicists have stumbled upon the same idea. Acoustic levitation is no longer fantasy; it is a growing field of study. With the right frequencies, tiny objects can be lifted, suspended, controlled.So I ask you , If we are only now rediscovering this knowledge, what else have we lost? Could it be that entire civilizations once harnessed sound , not as entertainment, but as technology? And if so, why was this knowledge buried?

Perhaps, because sound is not just creation. It is destruction too.

The music we surround ourselves with , from the deep, distorted bass of phonk to the refined elegance of classical, the vibrant pulse of afro beats, or the hypnotic rhythms of trance , doesn't just fill silence; it shapes us.

One striking example is the *Mozart Effect* ,a study that explored how classical music, particularly Mozart's compositions, could enhance cognitive function. In 1993, researchers at the University of California found that participants who listened to Mozart's Sonata for Two Pianos in D major showed improved spatial reasoning skills , a finding that sparked global interest in music's impact on the brain.

I decided to test this myself. One evening, feeling mentally drained, I played Mozart's Sonata . At first, it seemed like background noise , pleasant but unremarkable. Yet as the melody unfolded, something changed. My mind felt sharper, my thoughts more organized, as if my brain had found a rhythm to follow. Concepts I had struggled with suddenly seemed clearer, and tasks that once felt tedious became almost effortless.

On the other hand, studies have also explored the effects of darker, repetitive beats like those in phonk or heavy bass music. Research has shown that such low-frequency sounds can stimulate the brain's limbic system , the area responsible for emotions , potentially triggering aggression, anxiety, or even heightened focus depending on the listener's state of mind.

In contrast, Afro beats with their energetic, rhythmic patterns have been linked to improved mood and increased dopamine release, often encouraging movement and social connection.

The common thread? *Music is far more than background noise.* It's a force that can sharpen the mind, alter emotions, and even influence behavior , sometimes without us realizing it.

WHY DONT YOU TRY IT YOURSELF ? TODAY .

The Dancer is a Genius

“*"When you dance, you can enjoy the luxury of being you."*
— Paulo Coelho”

How Rhythm Rewires the Brain

What if every step you take, every sway of your body, is not just movement but an act of neurological alchemy? Science is only now catching up to what ancient civilizations already knew: movement and mind are not separate. The way we dance, the way we carry ourselves, the way we even gesture while speaking, all of it shapes our cognition, emotions, and even our perception of reality.

The Brain in Motion: The Neuroscience of Dance

Your body does not merely follow your mind,your mind follows your body. When you move with intention, when you dance, you trigger an intricate network of neurons spanning your motor cortex, cerebellum, and limbic system. But what's fascinating is how dance alters this network over time.

“*"The body says what words cannot."*
— Martha Graham”

Consider this,MRI scans of dancers reveal increased connectivity between the cerebellum and the prefrontal cortex, the very region responsible for creativity and problem-solving. A study on professional ballet dancers showed that their brains had superior proprioception, the ability to sense and control movement with extreme precision. But beyond physical coordination, these dancers exhibited heightened emotional intelligence and resilience to stress.

Why? Because dance is not just an art—it is embodied cognition. When we move rhythmically, we synchronize both hemispheres of the brain, allowing logic and intuition to work in harmony. The hippocampus, the brain's memory center, becomes more active. This is why dance therapy is now being used to treat Parkinson's disease, depression, and even trauma.

The Hidden Power of Rhythm

Music is not just sound. Rhythm is not just pattern. Both influence our autonomic nervous system, dictating heart rate, breath, and even hormonal release. The ancient Greeks believed in the concept of Ethos, the idea that different rhythms and melodies could shape one's character.

They were not wrong.Modern studies show that synchronizing movement with rhythm can alter brain chemistry. This is why warriors of old performed war dances before battle—to flood their systems with dopamine and adrenaline, sharpening focus and reducing fear. Why do people feel euphoric when dancing in unison at concerts? Because movement synchronized with beat stimulates the release of oxytocin, the "bonding hormone," creating an almost spiritual sense of unity.

But what happens when rhythm is disrupted? In 1950s CIA experiments, non-repetitive, erratic rhythms were used to induce confusion and mental breakdown in test subjects. Similarly, chaotic movement patterns in dance have been used in cult initiations, breaking down previous identities to implant new beliefs.

So, if rhythm and movement can strengthen the mind, can they also be used to manipulate it?

The Forbidden Science: Dance as a Key to Altered States

Many indigenous cultures have long known the connection between movement and consciousness. The Shamans of Siberia use rapid, repetitive movement to enter trance states, accessing information beyond ordinary perception. Whirling Dervishes, spinning endlessly in meditative ecstasy, claim to transcend the physical realm entirely.

What's even more mysterious is that science backs this up. In 2018, neuroscientists discovered that repetitive movement can alter the Default Mode Network (DMN)—the region of the brain responsible for self-awareness and ego. By disrupting the DMN, dancers report feelings of ego dissolution, where the boundaries between self and universe begin to blur.

Why do you think secret societies incorporated ritual dances? Why did ancient temples encode dance into their spiritual rites? Because they knew something we have forgotten.

Modern Applications: The Science of Power Postures

But you don't need to be a mystic or a shaman to use this knowledge. Even in daily life, movement shapes power. Studies show that expansive movements,holding your arms out, standing tall, occupying space ,trigger the release of testosterone and reduce cortisol, making you feel more confident and assertive. Meanwhile, closed-off postures, such as slouching or crossing your arms, can chemically make you feel powerless.

In business, in social interactions, in moments of fear—how you move dictates your reality.So the question is: if movement has the power to unlock the mind, shape emotions, and alter consciousness...

Who is truly in control? *ITS YOU* .

Personal Experience

There is a corner in my room , small, yet sacred , where the floor remembers every step I've carved into it. This is where I dance. Not for an audience, nor for applause, but for something far greater , to speak to the silence itself.

Here, I let my feet strike the earth with the fierce rhythm of flamenco, feeling the power through my veins . I flow with the grace of Odissi, each movement curling like whispered mantras and weaving stories . I sway in the serpentine elegance of Egyptian and Persian dances, feeling their ancient power coil through my spine. And when the night grows still, I glide through the softness of waltz, as if spinning through unseen constellations. Even hip-hop, bold and untamed, finds its place , a reminder that chaos too has rhythm.

But movement is not just art , it's identity. I danced the Nati of Himachal, steady and grounded like the mountains themselves. I felt the raw force of Bhangra, wild yet precise. The swift turns of Kathak taught me elegance in chaos, while the teasing rhythm of Lavani held a confidence that refused to be ignored.

I belong everywhere, yet nowhere. In this quiet corner , this forgotten temple — I have learned that dance is not mere movement. It is language. It is alchemy. Each step carries the weight of unspoken thoughts, and every twirl unveils a piece of the universe I hide within.

“*"I never learned to dance ,*
I only remembered." -as i once wrote, as Divyansa”

CHAPTER EIGHT

MACHINA

(Engineering the Impossible)

"Where the laws of nature bow to human will."

Art through lens of Science

AI-Generated Art vs. Human Creativity—Will Machines Replace Us, or Will They Expose New Dimensions?

Art has always been a distinctly human endeavor , fueled by emotion, intuition, and experience. But in the 21st century, artificial intelligence has entered the creative arena, producing paintings, music, poetry, and even choreographed dance. The question that lingers is not just whether AI can create art, but whether it can feel art. Does it imagine beyond our limitations?

{ The Birth of the Machine Artist }

In 2018, a portrait titled Edmond de Belamy was sold at Christie's for $432,500. The twist? It was not painted by human hands but by an algorithm trained on thousands of historical paintings. The AI, created by the Paris-based collective Obvious, had learned styles, textures, and brushstrokes, blending them into something eerily familiar yet unquestionably new.

Case Study: AI and the Lost Work of Rembrandt

A project called The Next Rembrandt trained an AI on over 300 of Rembrandt's paintings, analyzing brush techniques, compositions, and lighting. The AI then "painted" a brand-new Rembrandt-style artwork, something the Dutch master never actually created, yet one that bore his unmistakable signature style.

Does this mean AI can replace artists? Not quite. AI lacks the spontaneity of a Van Gogh stroke, the pain behind a Frida Kahlo self-portrait, the rebellious defiance of a Banksy mural. But what it offers is a mirror into our own patterns of creation, revealing subconscious elements that even we, the artists, may not see.

Consider the Chinese Room Argument, proposed by philosopher John Searle. If a machine processes language according to set rules, does it understand language, or is it merely following an algorithm? The same applies to AI-generated art, does it create or does it simply rearrange patterns it has learned?

The Difference Between Inspiration and Imitation

AI can replicate Monet's water lilies but has never gazed upon a pond at dawn, feeling the crisp air on its skin. AI can compose symphonies in Bach's style, but has never felt the heartbreak that led Beethoven to write his Moonlight Sonata. What AI does is expose patterns that we, as humans, overlook. It does not replace creativity, it augments it. It challenges us to redefine what it means to create, pushing us to explore beyond what we thought possible.

{ The Fusion of AI and Human Art—A New Renaissance? }

Case Study: AI as a Choreographer

In 2020, Google's DeepMind was used to generate new dance movements, choreographing performances based on music and existing dance styles. When real dancers performed these sequences, they were surprised, AI introduced unexpected transitions that a human choreographer might never have considered. The result? A fusion of machine precision and human fluidity which was entirely new. Imagine being able to create a new dance form with the help of AI.

Case Study: AI in Architecture

Zaha Hadid Architects have begun using AI to design buildings that push the limits of engineering, blending futuristic curves with natural flow. AI-driven generative design has allowed architects to experiment with structures that defy traditional constraints, much like how da Vinci sketched flying machines centuries before aerodynamics was understood.

The Ultimate Question: Can AI Dream?

The great artists of history were visionaries, but they were also rebels. They broke rules. They saw what others refused to see. AI, for all its computational power, does not yet know how to break rules. It does not feel longing, nostalgia, euphoria, or grief.

But perhaps its greatest role is not to replace us, but to show us where we have been blind. To reflect the very patterns that make us human and, in doing so, push us to go beyond them. Ands the real question is not whether AI can create, but whether it can teach us to create in ways we never imagined.

> “*"Because true genius lies not in what we create, but in what we awaken within ourselves — the questions we dare to ask, the limits we choose to break, and the visions we refuse to abandon."*”

The Physics of Impossible Sculptures

"In one of my readings , *The Science of Illusions* by Jacques Ninio , i discovered a curious truth. Some artists do not just imitate reality; they distort it...Art has long been a mirror to reality, but some artists choose to shatter that mirror, bending light, twisting perspectives, and challenging the very laws of physics. When you stand before an Anish Kapoor sculpture, gaze at an M.C. Escher print, or watch a kinetic masterpiece shift and move, you are witnessing a rebellion against natural order. But is it magic? No, it is science disguised as art.

M.C. Escher: The Architect of the Impossible

Maurits Cornelis Escher was not a scientist, yet his art has fascinated physicists and mathematicians for decades. His works seem to depict endless staircases, waterfalls that flow uphill, and rooms where gravity bends upon itself. But how did he achieve this illusion?

The Science Behind Escher's Paradoxes

The Penrose Triangle: Many of Escher's works, like Ascending and Descending, rely on the concept of impossible geometry, shapes that, while logically inconsistent in three dimensions, appear normal from certain perspectives. Horizon Distortion: Escher used warped vanishing points, an optical trick that forces the brain to misinterpret depth, making the impossible seem real. Tessellations & Fractals: His use of repeating patterns, inspired by crystallography, was later found to mirror quasi-crystals, which weren't scientifically confirmed until the 1980s.

Case Study: Waterfall (1961)

In this famous lithograph, water appears to flow uphill before cascading down again, forming an endless loop. The illusion works because of careful shading and forced perspective, tricking the brain into accepting an unnatural reality.

Anish Kapoor: Sculpting the Void

Where Escher defied perception, Anish Kapoor defies space itself. His sculptures manipulate light, reflection, and negative space, creating the illusion of infinite depth or impossible curvature.

The Science Behind Kapoor's Works

Vantablack, a material Kapoor controversially acquired exclusive rights to, is one of the blackest substances on Earth . When used in sculptures, it creates a void-like effect, making objects appear as if they don't exist at all. Concave Mirrors, in works like Cloud Gate (The Bean in Chicago), Kapoor uses highly reflective concave surfaces to distort reality, warping the city skyline into liquid-like reflections. Optical Infinity, some of his installations use mathematical curves known as hyperboloids, which interact with light in ways that eliminate shadows, making them appear two-dimensional from certain angles.

Case Study: Descension (2014)

This installation creates a swirling vortex of water that looks like a bottomless whirlpool. The trick? A hidden pump keeps the water moving, and dark colors make it hard to tell how deep it really is, leaving the viewer unsure if it's just a shallow pool or a true abyss.

Kinetic Art: When Physics and Sculpture Dance

Where Kapoor and Escher play with perception, kinetic artists take things a step further, introducing motion, time, and physics into their creations.

Jean Tinguely & the Art of Chaos

Known for his self-destructing sculptures, Tinguely designed mechanical artworks that seemed to operate with a mind of their own. Using principles of entropy and mechanical failure, his works illustrated the beauty of decay and impermanence.

Theo Jansen's Strandbeests—Walking Sculptures Powered by Wind

Jansen, a Dutch artist, engineers large-scale kinetic sculptures that "walk" using only the power of the wind. Inspired by natural selection, these machines use complex linkage systems based on fractal geometry, allowing them to move in eerily lifelike ways.

By refining designs over decades, Jansen's kinetic creatures have developed behaviors akin to living organisms. Some can even detect water and change direction to avoid sinking.

Beyond Illusion: The Future of Impossible Sculptures

Advancements in materials science and AI-driven engineering are pushing the boundaries of sculpture further than ever before,

- *Magnetism & Superconductors*—Some modern sculptures seem to defy gravity itself. Using quantum levitation, objects hover in midair, held up by invisible magnetic forces. What once seemed like magic is now a fusion of science and art, where materials float effortlessly, challenging our understanding of space and movement.One notable example is the installation Quantum Levitation by Israeli artist Eyal Gever, where metallic objects float eerily in midair, held in place by magnetic fields.

- *Shape Memory Alloys*—These sculptures change shape over time, reacting to temperature or touch. Made from special metals that "remember" their original form, they shift and bend as if alive. No longer just frozen in time, they evolve, making the viewer question whether art is something fixed or something that breathes.In Morphogenesis, a sculpture by artist Jonty Hurwitz, strands of alloy metal twist and reshape themselves in response to touch, creating a sense of movement and transformation that mirrors living organisms.
- *Augmented Reality Sculptures*—Here, the physical and digital worlds merge. With the help of technology, static sculptures transform, overlaid with moving images, lights, and interactive elements. These works are never the same twice, each experience is unique, shaped by the viewer and the moment.In 2020, a team at the Massachusetts Museum of Contemporary Art (MASS MoCA) collaborated with digital artists to create Invisible Cities, an AR installation that allows visitors to view shifting digital landscapes layered over physical sculptures.

Final Thought: Are We Sculpting the Future?

Throughout history, artists have sought ways to cheat nature,not by defying its laws, but by mastering them. They have bent light to craft illusions, manipulated motion to warp time, and even played with magnetic fields to suspend objects in midair. From the perfect symmetry of Da Vinci's Vitruvian Man to Escher's impossible staircases, from Kapoor's voids that swallow perception to kinetic sculptures that dance with the wind,each creation challenges what we accept as reality.

But as we push the boundaries of perception, a more unsettling question emerges: If reality can be so effortlessly distorted, was it ever truly fixed to begin with? If the mind can be tricked, if the eye can be deceived, then what separates the tangible from the imagined? Perhaps we are merely sculpting illusions, or have we always lived within one?

Yet, this interplay between art and science reveals something even more profound. When an artist thinks like an engineer, they gain the power to shape the impossible, structures that defy gravity, installations that bend sound, and paintings that breathe life. And when an engineer thinks like an artist, they see beyond equations, they design bridges that resemble poetry, machines that dance with elegance, and technology that feels almost alive.

Art is not just a reflection of reality, but the very act of rewriting it. And if that is true ,then how much of the world around us is not what it seems, but what we choose to believe .

A Note to the Geniuses I Seek

I want artists to become great engineers of their craft , to create art that cannot be denied by logic, yet when analyzed, reveals infinite layers of knowledge. Art that stands as proof that creativity is not chaos, but calculated mastery. I want engineers to become great artists , to build structures that seem impossible to the human brain, that lure the eyes that see, that make even the gods marvel at what humans are capable of.

In fact, I believe God is a mindset , a state of being where mastery, creation, and vision align. Not everyone will agree. Not everyone will understand. Because belief is personal and that's what makes humanity so deeply beautiful.

But for those who understand, the visionaries, the innovators, the quiet minds that carry storms within — *I want you to be part of my world.*

No... *I want you to be part of my empire.*

The Future of Light as an Art Form

Holograms, Bio-Luminescence, and Paintings That Move

Light is the first artist. Before hands sculpted clay or pigments stained the walls of caves, light had already carved the heavens into day and night, shadow and brilliance. It was the brushstroke of the divine, shaping the world long before humans learned to imitate its mastery.

For centuries, we have chased it, worshipped it, bent it to our will. We built stained-glass windows that bled color into cathedrals, painted illusions that mimicked its deception, and ignited candles to defy the darkness. But what happens when light is no longer just a tool for art, but the very essence of it?

We stand at the threshold of a new era, where canvases breathe, shadows are no longer silent, and paintings defy stillness. The art of tomorrow will not be framed and hung upon a wall. It will glow, shift, and dance with the motion of the viewer, whispering secrets in wavelengths unseen. The future of art is no longer bound by pigment or permanence. *The future of art is light.*

The Phantom Reality of Holograms

What is real? A question pondered by philosophers, physicists, and poets alike. A hologram is a paradox, a thing that exists and does not exist, a ghost made of light, a mirage with no substance. Yet, in its illusion lies its power.

To understand a hologram is to understand deception itself. Unlike a traditional image, which captures a reflection of reality, a hologram encodes the nature of light, storing the shape, depth, and movement of an object as if it were frozen in space. It does not imitate life; it recreates it.There have already been attempts to summon the dead with this sorcery of science. Tupac Shakur walked onstage in 2012, years after his death. Maria Callas sang once more in an opera house, her voice untouched by time. But these are only echoes of what is to come. What happens when an artist no longer paints a portrait, but creates a presence? When a museum no longer holds artifacts, but resurrects emperors?

Will we stand before a glowing Da Vinci, watching him perfect the strokes of a Mona Lisa that shifts under his hands? And if we do,if we come face to face with history woven in light, will it still be history? Perhaps we will have rewritten it .

The Glow of Living Art: Bio-Luminescence and the Paintings That Breathe

Somewhere in the depths of the ocean, a creature drifts through the black void, leaving behind a shimmering trail of green and blue ,a fire that burns without heat, a light that comes from within.Nature has known the secret of self-illumination for millennia, long before the first torch was ever lit. Fireflies signal through the darkness. Algae glow upon the crests of waves. Certain mushrooms radiate an strange luminescence in forgotten forests. And now, we have stolen their secret.

What if a painting could glow without electricity? What if a sculpture pulsed, alive with its own bioluminescent rhythm? Scientists have already engineered plants that emit light like fireflies, their leaves shimmering faintly in the dark. Artists have begun to grow paintings, microbial masterpieces, where bacteria bloom into luminous patterns, shifting and changing with time.

A world without artificial light is not a world of darkness, but a world where the art around us breathes, glows, and responds, a world *where nature itself is the canvas.*

The Death of Stillness: When Paintings Refuse to Stay Silent

A painting has always been a moment trapped in time. A frozen expression, a single thought preserved in oils and pigment, locked within the confines of a frame. But what if it was no longer still? Imagine if art could shift, evolve, and change. Technology has already begun to peel away the stillness. Thermochromic inks allow paintings to reveal hidden layers when touched. Digital canvases now adapt to the emotions of the viewer. AI-generated works can reassemble themselves, shifting their composition like a dream that refuses to be pinned down.

Imagine standing before a portrait that knows you, one that shifts its gaze, responding to the rhythm of your heartbeat. Imagine a fresco that erases itself at dawn and is reborn each night, its colors blooming anew with the setting sun. The very idea unsettles us. We are accustomed to art that listens but does not speak, that watches but does not move. If paintings learn to breathe, if they learn to think,do they cease to be paintings? Or do they become something else entirely?

And if art no longer needs an artist to be born, if creation no longer requires a creator, do we, the artists, still exist at all? And when I say artists, I'm speaking to *you — yes, you, the reader*. It doesn't matter what you do; you are an artist. Whether your life feels vibrant or dull, chaotic or calm , you've shaped it. Even if you believe you've created *nothing*,that belief itself is a creation. The way you wake up, the thoughts you repeat, the choices you make , all of it is your canvas.

And if you don't believe me, that's exactly how you're shaping your *now. Rethink it.*

The Final Light

For centuries, we have shaped light to serve us. We have caged it in lanterns, bent it through glass, demanded that it paint our world in color. But the future we are entering is one where light is no longer our servant, it is our successor. Holograms will create worlds that never existed. Bio-luminescence will bring forth art that is alive. Moving paintings will refuse to be captured by time.

And so, *I ask you*, When our creations can shift, glow, and move at will, when light itself has become the artist, *have we illuminated the world, or have we become the ghosts within it?*

CHAPTER NINE

GENOME

(Art in Your DNA)

"The brushstrokes of ancestry, the blueprint of genius."

Codes of the Ancients in Blood

> *"The blood remembers what the mind forgets." — N.K. Jemisin, The Broken Earth Trilogy*

There are whispers in your bones, echoes in your blood. The artist, the scientist, the madman, they are not separate creatures, but reflections of the same spark. A fire passed down through the ages, carried in the delicate strands of DNA that weave your existence.

Art is not merely learned. It is inherited. It is carved into the double helix of your being, a ghostly signature of those who came before you. A genetic memory of cave painters who smeared ochre onto rock walls, of astronomers who traced constellations into parchment, of composers who heard symphonies before the first note was played.

Creativity is no accident. The ability to sculpt, paint, write, and invent is embedded deep within your molecular code, waiting to be deciphered. The same DNA that births genius is the one that whispers insanity. *"For history has shown us—there is no brilliance without madness."*

The Blueprint of the Gifted and the Cursed

Leonardo da Vinci dissected corpses at night, sketching the hidden architecture of the human body by candlelight, his mind forever split between science and beauty.
Van Gogh cut off his own ear, painting swirls of madness in a sky that only he could see.
Tesla spoke to pigeons and feared the sight of pearls, his mind crackling with visions of light before they could be realized.Is it coincidence that the greatest artists, the most visionary scientists,

walked the fine edge between genius and destruction? Or is there a pattern, a code, an unspoken law that binds brilliance to torment.

Recent studies suggest that creativity and mental instability are not merely linked ,they are written into the very fabric of our DNA. Researchers have found that those with artistic and scientific gifts often share genetic markers associated with bipolar disorder, schizophrenia, and heightened neural connectivity. The same mutations that allow the mind to see beyond the ordinary, to create, to innovate, also leave it vulnerable to chaos, obsession, and breakdown.

To be a creator is to gamble with one's own sanity.

The Ancient Bloodline of Creation

Before neuroscience, before genetics, before we understood what lay inside our cells, civilizations already sensed the connection. The Greeks called it the divine madness of the Muses. The Renaissance called it genius. The Romantics called it torment.

Pharaohs of Egypt commissioned temples not just for gods, but for mathematicians and artists, believing *that creation itself was a sacred act*, a gift passed through *royal bloodlines.* The Chinese dynasties traced poetry through family lineage, believing that *talent was an inherited force.*

And now, modern science has only confirmed what the ancients suspected, ***art runs through bloodlines.***Studies on identical twins separated at birth reveal eerie similarities in their creative pursuits, one a painter in Europe, the other an architect in America, their genetic code guiding them toward the same obsession. Families of composers, generations of sculptors, dynasties of thinkers,all linked by invisible threads of inheritance.

Even today, when a child picks up a brush, a violin, or a microscope, we do not ask where the gift came from. We say, "It runs in the family."

The Gene That Dreams in Color

But what is this force within us? What is the genetic key that unlocks vision beyond the ordinary? Scientists have begun mapping the genetic foundation of creativity, tracing it to specific mutations in genes related to dopamine regulation, neural plasticity, and cognitive flexibility. These genes allow for, Hyperconnectivity in the brain, where distant regions communicate in ways they do not in ordinary minds. Increased pattern recognition, the ability to see structure where others see noise. Heightened emotional sensitivity, allowing an artist to feel the world with unbearable intensity.

But there is a cost. These same genes are also linked to mental fragility, hallucinations, obsession, and mood instability. To create is to open doors within the mind that were never meant to be unlocked. Some walk through unscathed. *Others do not return.*

What do you think? Will you?

The Curse of the Gifted

History is filled with artists who drowned in their own visions. Writers who fell into madness, mathematicians who lost themselves in spirals of numbers, painters who saw too much, felt too much, broke under the weight of creation.

Virginia Woolf walked into a river, her pockets filled with stones. Edgar Allan Poe drank himself to death, haunted by nightmares he could not escape. Kurt Cobain, a poet in the language of sound, left behind a note that whispered, "It's better to burn out than to fade away."

They were not weak. They were not lost. They were vessels, *born with the gift, cursed with the weight of it.*

The Future of Creativity: Can We Alter the Artist's DNA?

Now, with the rise of genetic engineering, we stand at the edge of a question once unthinkable-If we could edit out the madness from the artist, would we still have the art? Imagine a world where we could isolate the gene responsible for brilliance but remove its darker twin. A world where a Van Gogh could paint without pain, a Tesla could invent without obsession, a Poe could write without sorrow. Would their art remain? Would the fire still burn, or would we extinguish it with our precision.

Perhaps, in our quest to understand creativity, we risk destroying it. Or perhaps the answer is not in altering the artist, but in understanding them. To be a creator is to walk the edge of chaos. The question is—*will you play with it or fall?*

"Epigenetics: Can 'You' Be Passed Through Generations?

You were born with stories etched into your cells. Not just your mother's eyes or your father's hands, but something deeper—an inheritance of fire and shadow, a history of emotions passed down like an unspoken curse or blessing.

> "*As Carl Jung once wrote, 'The meeting of two personalities is like the contact of two chemical substances: if there is any reaction, both are transformed.' Perhaps the same is true within us — a fusion of ancestral echoes shaping who we become."*"

The artist does not emerge from nothing. The scientist does not discover in isolation. They carry the weight of those who came before them,their passions, their obsessions, their wounds. But is this inheritance merely cultural, or does it reside in the very structure of our DNA?

Science now suggests that the pain of your ancestors, the triumphs of your lineage, and the creative brilliance of those before you are not just memories locked in history. They are encoded into the genes that shape you. This is the science of *epigenetics* , the study of how experiences, especially extreme ones, can alter genetic expression and be passed down through generations.

If trauma leaves marks on the body, what does it do to the mind? If passion fuels an artist's creation, does it echo in their descendants? Let us decipher the silent language of inheritance.

The Science Behind Memory in Blood

For centuries, poets have written of bloodlines, of ancestral curses, of destiny written in one's very being. They were not entirely wrong. Your DNA is not a fixed script, it is a living manuscript, rewritten by life itself. Epigenetics reveals that your genetic code is not the only factor shaping you. The experiences of your ancestors—famine, war, love, loss, leave molecular scars on DNA, modifying how genes are expressed without altering their sequence. These modifications, known as epigenetic marks, can silence or activate certain traits, carrying emotional and psychological imprints across generations.

Consider this,

The Holocaust and War Trauma

Studies have shown that descendants of Holocaust survivors exhibit heightened stress responses, altered cortisol levels, and an increased risk of anxiety and PTSD. The trauma did not die with the survivors, it left molecular imprints on their children's genes.

The Dutch Hunger Winter (1944-45)

A famine struck the Netherlands during World War II. Decades later, researchers found that children born to malnourished mothers had permanent changes in metabolism and increased risks of disease effects that lasted for generations. Their bodies had been programmed to endure starvation, even though they themselves had never known hunger.

African American Slavery and Generational Pain

Scientists have begun exploring the possibility that the long history of enslavement, oppression, and systemic suffering has left epigenetic marks on Black communities, potentially influencing stress-related illnesses and resilience factors even today.

If suffering is encoded into the body, is passion also? If trauma is inherited, can genius be?

The Epigenetics of the Artist's Mind

If war, starvation, and oppression can leave genetic marks, then so can the fevered passion of creation. The obsessive nature of a composer, the fire of a poet, and the innovation of a scientist may be passed through bloodlines, shaping future generations of visionaries. And some of the greatest creative lineages prove that .

The Bach Family of Composers

Over 50 musicians, spanning generations, emerged from the Bach family, culminating in Johann Sebastian Bach. Was this merely upbringing, or did musical intuition flow in their blood?

The Darwins & The Wedgewoods

Charles Darwin's family tree was an empire of thinkers. His grandfather Erasmus Darwin was a scientist and poet; his cousin Francis Galton pioneered eugenics. Did a genetic predisposition for curiosity and intellectual obsession shape the mind of the man who would unravel evolution itself?

The Brontë Sisters

Three women—Charlotte, Emily, and Anne,who, despite their isolation on the Yorkshire moors, became literary legends. Their father, a poet. Their childhood filled with elaborate storytelling. A coincidence, or an inherited hunger for words?

Perhaps the fire that makes an artist burn is something more than learned,it is encoded, a trait *sculpted by ancestors who dreamed before them.*

The Double-Edged Sword of Inherited Passion

But creativity, like all inherited gifts, comes with a cost. The same epigenetic traits that may enhance artistic vision could also heighten vulnerability to depression, addiction, and mental instability. The ancestral genius that fuels brilliance may also predispose one to suffering.

Ernest Hemingway stood among the literary giants of the 20th century, his prose as sharp as the life he lived. But behind the brilliance lurked a darkness that ran deep in his bloodline. His father, sister, brother, and granddaughter all succumbed to the same tragic fate—suicide. The same force that fueled his creative fire seemed to have scorched the mind that carried it.

Pyotr Ilyich Tchaikovsky composed with a soul laid bare,sweeping, aching, unrelenting. His music carried the weight of something vast, something consuming. He suffered from violent mood swings, from melancholia that threatened to drown him. His brother, Modest, a writer, shared these traits. The brilliance that poured from their minds seemed to come at a cost, *one measured in quiet despair.*

Perhaps genius and madness are two sides of the same inherited coin.

Unlocking the Creative Code

If creativity, passion, and even suffering are encoded within us, the question arises, Can we harness this inheritance? Can we awaken dormant creative genes, or silence the burdens of trauma?

Neuroplasticity & Creative Training

Just as epigenetic markers can be passed down, they can also be altered in one's own lifetime. Studies show that engaging in artistic pursuits, music, dance, writing—can rewire neural pathways, potentially awakening dormant genetic potentials inherited from artistic ancestors.

Mindfulness & Genetic Healing

Meditation, mindfulness, and deep creative immersion have been shown to alter gene expression, reducing stress markers and potentially reversing negative epigenetic modifications. In other words, you can rewrite the genetic scars of the past.

The Future of Epigenetic Engineering

What if we could enhance the genes associated with creativity while suppressing those linked to self-destruction? Could the next Mozart or da Vinci be genetically cultivated, designed to create without suffering? Or would we risk losing the very thing that makes genius so raw, so powerful, so human?

The answer is unknown. But one truth remains—*your art is older than you.* It is written in your bones, whispered in your blood, carried in the silent language of your DNA. You are not simply an artist. You are a vessel for generations of vision, pain, and passion. What will you do with it? After closing this page, this book, what will you do?

The pages close, but the truth does not. What comes next is already in you.

Unlocking the Forgotten Power of the Ancients

You may not know their names. You may never trace their footsteps, never see their faces carved into fading stone or written in lost records. But they are in you.

The warriors, the poets, the shamans who once walked the earth, who sang under the moon, who wove spells into melodies, who built civilizations with their bare hands, *they did not vanish*. They live in the blood that rushes through your veins, in the way your mind sparks with curiosity, in the restless fire that refuses to let you be ordinary.

But how do we awaken their power when history has erased them? How do we summon the knowledge in our cells when we do not even know what it is we have lost? This is where science and the forgotten arts collide.

The Lost Science of Blood Memory

For years, history was thought of as something external, written records, artifacts, ruins left behind. But what if history is also internal? What if it was never lost, just sleeping?

Epigenetics has proven that trauma, resilience, even skills, and fears can be passed down through generations. The question is, can we awaken the knowledge buried within us? If you were born into a family that never painted, never composed, never studied the stars, does that mean you have no ancestral link to art, to music, to science? No. Because you are the sum of a thousand forgotten lives. Their experiences did not vanish; they merely lay dormant, waiting for the right key to unlock them.

And *there are ways to do it*. Ancient ways. Scientific ways. The world just forgot.

Reactivating the Genetic Codes of the Ancients

I've spent a while figuring this out. It's not one clear path, but a series of activations.

The Triggers of the Forgotten Mind—Ritual, Sound, and Movement
Ancient civilizations did not pass knowledge through books alone. They coded it into rituals, into music, into the way they moved their bodies. Why does a particular rhythm stir something deep inside you, a language beyond words? Why do specific frequencies induce trances, unlock memories, make the skin shiver as if something unseen just recognized you? This is not fantasy. Sound alters the brain's electromagnetic field, shifting it into states where memory, *ancestral memory*,becomes accessible.

Binaural beats and ancient chants are more than just sounds, they're frequencies that tune the brain like an instrument. Certain tones can sync both hemispheres, opening doors to creativity, intuition, and forgotten knowledge that lingers beneath the surface.

Drumming and rhythmic movement have been used for centuries by shamans seeking wisdom. Science now shows that these steady beats create theta brain waves, the same state where intuition sharpens, memories resurface, and the mind drifts into deeper understanding.

Then there's dance, a language older than words. It's not just movement; it's a kind of remembering. Indigenous dances, martial arts, even the poised grace of Kathak or Tai Chi, they stir something deeper. These aren't just steps, they're codes, unlocking energy channels that have been asleep for generations.

Personal Experiment,

I tested this. I immersed myself in sounds that can't be described, moved in ways that can't be explained and something happened.I began dreaming of places I had never been, seeing symbols I had never learned, feeling emotions that belonged to another time.

Your body remembers even when your mind does not. Its strange but its true.

The Science of Awakening Dormant Traits

See, the key to unlocking genetic knowledge isn't just the external stimulation, but how we train our minds and bodies.

Ancient mystics fasted not for punishment, but to reset the body's energy and activate dormant DNA. In 2016, Japanese scientist Yoshinori Ohsumi was awarded the Nobel Prize for his groundbreaking research on *autophagy*, the body's process of cellular renewal. During fasting, cells break down damaged components, clearing outdated genetic data and optimizing brain function. This regenerative process not only promotes longevity but may also unlock deeper mental clarity, perhaps explaining why sages, monks, and mystics embraced fasting as a path to heightened awareness. What once seemed like spiritual discipline is now understood as biological precision, *an ancient key to unlocking the body's hidden intelligence.*

The body, when pushed into extreme environments (cold water, intense heat), triggers survival genes—many of which have not been activated for generations.Wim Hof, often called *The Iceman*, demonstrated this through controlled exposure to extreme cold. Using breath control and meditation, he achieved feats once thought impossible, like climbing Mount Kilimanjaro in shorts and withstanding prolonged ice immersion. Studies at Radboud

University confirmed that Hof's techniques allowed him to consciously influence his autonomic nervous system, activating immune responses previously believed to be involuntary. Nordic and Tibetan monks practiced this for centuries. Now, modern biohackers are proving that these techniques awaken latent physical and mental capacities.

Many cultures believed dreams were a gateway to ancestral knowledge. Now, studies show that lucid dreaming enhances neural plasticity, allowing access to deeper layers of memory and intuition. Could this be a lost technology of the mind? Nikola Tesla often spoke of vivid dream states where ideas seemed to unfold on their own. Srinivasa Ramanujan claimed that mathematical insights appeared to him in visions. Even artists like Salvador Dalí used controlled dream states to unlock their imagination. I've found answers in dreams, things I couldn't have known, yet somehow did. Pieces of hidden knowledge surfaced, not as thoughts, but as something deeper, felt, understood, and absolute.

You won't grasp this by simply reading about it. You have to step into it. You have to *try for yourself*. Only then will you see what your mind has been trying to tell you all along.

Language & Symbols—Reconnecting with Lost Intelligence

Every civilization encoded its greatest secrets into symbols. Why? Because symbols bypass logic and speak directly to the subconscious. Ever felt drawn to a particular ancient script, a sigil, a geometric form? It is not random. Your mind recognizes something your history books do not.

Ancient symbols are more than markings on stone, they are language etched into the subconscious. Neuroscience reveals that these symbols activate regions of the brain untouched by modern alphabets, as if the mind recognizes something far older, something woven into its very structure. Some researchers believe this response is more than coincidence. It suggests a deeper, instinctual recognition, a silent conversation between the self and the symbols that shaped civilizations.

Sacred geometry follows this same pattern. Pyramids, mandalas, fractals, these designs appear across cultures and epochs, not by chance, but because they mirror something fundamental. They reflect the natural coding of the universe, repeating patterns that spiral through galaxies, seashells, and strands of DNA. To see these forms is to witness a language we were never taught, yet somehow understand—a reminder that within us lies the same quiet order, waiting to be remembered.

The Forgotten Path of Self-Discovery

You do not need to know your ancestors' names to access their knowledge. You do not need to trace your lineage to awaken the gifts in your blood. The techniques exist. The science confirms it. The ancients knew it. It is about reactivation, not just learning. Your body holds their strength. Train it. Your mind holds their knowledge. Stimulate it.Your intuition holds their memory. Trust it.

The question is—*are you willing to unlock what has been hidden?*

Rewriting DNA: Can We Sculpt Ourselves Without Surgery?

Perfection is not a myth—it is a code. The human body, at its core, is not a fixed structure but a shifting sequence of genetic instructions, a biological symphony that adapts, mutates, and evolves. If we can decode the rhythm of this symphony, if we can learn its language, then what stops us from rewriting it? Not in a laboratory, not under a surgeon's knife, but within ourselves, through knowledge, practice, and understanding of the silent forces that govern biology.

This is not theory. This is truth. I have tried, and not only I, many have. Some known, others forgotten, each reaching beyond the limits they were told could not be crossed. Their stories remain scattered, whispered through time, but they exist. Beyond records, beyond recognition, proof that the mind, the body, and the spirit are far more powerful than we have been led to believe.

For centuries, science and mysticism have moved in parallel, both seeking the same truth but speaking different languages. What the ancients called alchemy, modern genetics calls epigenetics. What was once ritual is now biohacking. But the core idea remains, *the body is not static*, and transformation is not only possible but inevitable for those who know how to command it.

The Science of Self-Alteration: Beyond Genetic Editing

The modern world tells us that to change our appearance, we must submit, to genetics, to plastic surgery, to external forces that mold us. But what if the ability to sculpt ourselves lies within? The answer is not in editing the genes themselves but in rewriting their instructions.

Epigenetic Reprogramming: The Invisible Hand of Change
Genes do not work in isolation. They are switches, turning on and off in response to stimuli—what we eat, how we think, the environment we place ourselves in. Scientists have already proven that fasting activates longevity genes, that stress alters DNA expression, that childhood trauma imprints itself at the genetic level. If the body reacts to external forces, then can we not deliberately apply the right pressures to shape ourselves?

DNA Methylation & Histone Modification: These are the biological mechanisms that dictate gene expression. They are influenced by diet, sleep, movement, and even intention. The right chemical triggers, found in specific foods, herbs, and even breathing techniques—*can modify how genes behave.*

Hormonal Manipulation: Testosterone, estrogen, HGH—these are the sculptors of bone structure, skin texture, and muscle composition. But they do not act alone. They respond to neurotransmitters, to micro-nutritional cues, to cycles of fasting and feasting. Understanding this interplay means understanding how to change one's very form.

Bioelectricity: The Body's Hidden Code
Cells communicate through electrical currents. The nervous system is an intricate circuit, sending signals that dictate healing, growth, and form. If these signals can be hacked, altered, or amplified, then body modification becomes an internal process, not an external one.

The Levin Experiments: Reprogramming Life Through Bioelectricity

Dr. Michael Levin's pioneering work in bioelectricity is reshaping what we know about cellular behavior. His research reveals that cells communicate not only through chemical signals but also through electrical patterns,an overlooked language that directs growth, repair, and form. In one of Levin's most striking experiments, frogs that cannot naturally regenerate limbs in adulthood, were induced to regrow functional legs. This was achieved not through gene editing or surgery, but by manipulating the bioelectric code that guides cellular organization. By altering the electrical gradients across cell membranes, Levin's team reactivated dormant regenerative pathways, prompting the cells to behave as if they were in the early stages of limb development.

This discovery suggests that the body's blueprint may be more flexible than previously believed , a pattern of electric patterns shaping us from within. If limbs can be regrown through bioelectric modulation, what else might be possible? Could facial features, jawlines, cheekbones, even skin texture ,be subtly influenced by adjusting the bioelectric code of the skin? Emerging studies hint that controlled electrical stimulation may enhance tissue repair, collagen production, and even reshape soft facial contours.

The Silent Signals of Technology: Could Screens Be Reshaping Us?

If bioelectricity holds the power to regenerate limbs, what happens when our bodies are constantly exposed to uncontrolled electrical signals? Computers, phones, and digital devices emit low-frequency electromagnetic fields (EMFs) , invisible pulses of energy that surround us every day. While these signals are far weaker than the intentional bioelectric patterns used in regenerative research, their constant presence raises questions.

Dr. Andrew Marino, a pioneer in bioelectromagnetics, explored how weak electromagnetic fields affect biological systems. His research suggested that prolonged exposure to certain EMF frequencies can disrupt cellular communication, particularly in tissues sensitive to electrical signaling like the skin and nervous system. Cells rely on precise electrical gradients to regulate growth, repair, and structural alignment. If bioelectric patterns influence how facial tissues regenerate and adapt, it's possible that chaotic EMF signals though unintended could subtly interfere with these processes.

Some studies have proposed links between prolonged screen exposure and Collagen degradation, contributing to premature aging. Mitochondrial stress, which weakens cellular energy production. Circulatory changes, potentially affecting skin tone and texture.

This isn't to say screens are silently sculpting our faces but rather that the body's delicate electrical balance may be shifting in ways we have yet to fully understand.

Sound Frequencies & Cellular Resonance: The Science of Vibration

Ancient cultures believed sound could heal, transform, and unlock higher consciousness. Today, modern science is beginning to understand why. Studies in cymatics—the science of visible sound vibrations show that sound frequencies organize particles into intricate geometric patterns. This suggests that sound doesn't just move through the body; *it shapes it.*

In groundbreaking research, Dr. Guy Berthoumieux demonstrated that specific frequencies influence cellular organization. His work revealed that sound vibrations could guide cells into structured formations, much like the patterns seen in cymatic experiments. Meanwhile, bioresonance therapies are exploring the impact of sound on biological processes. Research has shown that certain frequencies may stimulate collagen synthesis, improve bone density, and accelerate cellular repair. Frequencies in the 30-50 Hz range, for example, have been linked to enhanced osteoblast activity, promoting stronger bones and improved facial structure.

In practice, this means the ancient belief in sound's transformative power may have a scientific foundation. The right frequencies may indeed refine jawlines, tighten skin, and awaken dormant regenerative pathways acting not just on the mind, but on the very structure of the body itself.

What Levin's frogs, cymatic studies, and modern technology suggest is profound that our bodies are not rigid structures but adaptable symphonies of energy and vibration. By learning to influence these silent codes whether through bioelectric signals, sound frequencies, or even by controlling our digital environment ,we may *unlock potentials once thought impossible.*

Lost Knowledge: The Forbidden Sciences of Self-Transformation

Science has its limits and not because the truth isn't there, but because it refuses to look where ancient minds once did. The idea of bodily transformation without surgery is not new. It exists in hidden manuscripts, in the forgotten corridors of knowledge.

The Yogic Bone Reshaping Practices

In obscure Sanskrit texts, there are mentions of rishis who reshaped their faces, elongated their limbs, refined their features , not through surgery, but through concentrated internal practices. The key lay in pranic manipulation, the control of vital energy to influence tissue growth.

Nasya Therapy & Facial Reconfiguration

Ayurvedic practitioners understood that certain herbal formulations, when inhaled correctly, could subtly alter nasal cartilage and facial structure over time. The principle? Targeted epigenetic influence through biochemical triggers.

Marma Point Activation

Specific pressure points on the face and skull, when manipulated correctly, were believed to stimulate growth and reshaping over time. Modern myofascial release techniques may be rediscovering this lost practice.

The Hermetic Principle of As Within, So Without

Hermeticists believed that reality, including the body, is a projection of internal states. This is not metaphorical , modern science is slowly catching up to the fact that perception alters biology.

The Observer Effect in Biology: If quantum mechanics states that observation changes reality, could self-perception influence physical form? Studies on neuroplasticity suggest that visualization can lead to real structural brain changes. Why not the body as well? *The Taoist Bone-Breathing Technique*: An ancient technique that suggested breathing in specific ways could direct energy to bones, subtly influencing their shape over time.

The Future: A New Science of Aesthetic Evolution

If we strip away limitations, if we merge the lost sciences with modern biohacking, what becomes possible? The future of aesthetic transformation is not in hospitals, but in laboratories of the self. The key is not in accepting of genetic as fate but it's about learning to work with the forces that shape us.

We are not static beings. We are written in code, and code—when understood—*can be rewritten*. This isn't just speculation. *This is a roadmap for those who dare to step beyond what is known*. Are you one of them?

<u>*A Personal Note*</u> -

I've often thought about what Achilles believed , that b*eauty was more than just appearance*; it was a reflection of strength, honor, and the soul itself. Plato once wrote that *beauty stirs the mind toward truth*, while Aristotle saw it as the harmony between form and purpose. The Greeks knew that to refine the body was to refine the spirit, a belief that shaped warriors, artists, and thinkers alike.

Beauty has always mattered to me. And let's be honest—it matters to you too. Who doesn't admire beauty? It speaks of care, discipline, and the life we choose to live. Everyone carries beauty within them, but few take the steps to reveal it. Those who do are the ones we call beautiful or handsome—the ones who dared to become what they were meant to be.

You may believe that beauty should come from within and of course, it should. But here's the truth, beauty on the outside is a choice. By choosing to refine yourself, to build strength, grace, and presence, you reveal more than just your features you reveal your discipline, your determination, and your mindset.

"*As Oscar Wilde once said, "It is only shallow people who do not judge by appearances. The true mystery of the world is the visible, not the invisible."*"

Outer beauty isn't vanity, it's a reflection of the effort you've poured into becoming your most powerful self. I dream of a world where beauty thrives not just in faces, but in actions, in thoughts, in the way people carry themselves. A world where elegance is not forgotten, where grace holds power, and where we choose to become not just good—*but breathtaking.*

AND REMEMBER ITS YOUR CHOICE !

Relationship Between Art and DNA

"The body is the instrument of the mind, and the mind is the architect of the body." — Leon Battista Alberti

Art and DNA share a fundamental truth , they are both codes of creation. Just as a painter manipulates colors on a canvas, or a sculptor refines form from stone, our genetic blueprint is a dynamic composition that can be altered, reshaped, and refined. The essence of art lies in transformation, in seeing potential where others see permanence. If we view DNA as an artistic medium rather than a fixed script, then self-reinvention becomes a creative act rather than a clinical procedure. Ancient traditions have long used visualizations, sacred geometry, and rhythmic practices,artistic expressions, to influence biological states. Could art, in its many forms, be the missing key to unlocking deeper genetic potential? Possibly yes.

Can Art Be Used to Reidentify DNA Changes?

Yes, and in multiple ways. Art, often seen as a form of self-expression, may in fact reach deeper, altering not just thoughts and emotions but influencing the very code that shapes us. Emerging research suggests that visual patterns, sound vibrations, and even physical movement may have the power to stimulate epigenetic shifts ,changes in gene expression without altering the DNA sequence itself.

Visual Stimulation & Gene Activation

The idea that colors, patterns, and visual designs can influence biology is not new. Cultures have long used sacred geometry, mandalas, and fractal patterns in their spiritual practices , forms that seem to hold a mysterious power. Modern science is now exploring why.

Studies in neuroaesthetics reveal that exposure to certain geometric patterns activates regions of the brain linked to relaxation, creativity, and even cellular repair. Fractals, repeating patterns found in nature, have shown remarkable effects on stress reduction and neural coherence. Researchers have found that viewing fractals can reduce cortisol levels by up to 60%, supporting the theory that our biology responds to visual harmony.

But deeper than relaxation, visual patterns may influence gene expression itself. Some researchers suggest that symmetrical patterns, by promoting mental calm and balance, can alter the body's methylation process, a key mechanism in epigenetics that silences or activates genes. This aligns with the theory that ancient symbols like yantras, labyrinths, and mandalas may carry encoded triggers for subconscious biological responses.

Sonic Influence on Cellular Structures

Sound is vibration and vibration moves through the body, influencing molecular structure. Research in cymatics has shown that sound frequencies create distinct geometric patterns in substances like sand, water, and even cells. This suggests that sound waves may have the potential to organize biological systems at a molecular level.

Sound's influence on the nervous system may extend to genetic expression as well. By activating the vagus nerve, certain sounds can reduce inflammation, balance hormones, and trigger epigenetic responses related to stress, immunity, and even skin health.

Physical Expression as Epigenetic Influence

Movement is not just mechanical, it's deeply tied to biology. Certain forms of dance, martial arts, and ritualistic movements engage muscles, fascia, and even bones in a way that may influence DNA expression.

Biomechanical researchers have explored how myokines, proteins released during muscle movement, act as genetic messengers. These molecules can influence metabolism, mood, and even neuroplasticity. Some believe that carefully designed movement patterns such as those seen in yoga asanas or qigong flows may activate dormant genetic codes by aligning breath, posture, and energetic flow.

Symbolic Representation in Genetic Encoding

The notion that symbols could directly influence DNA may seem mystical, yet some researchers believe there's more to it. Ancient glyphs, runes, and sigils often follow precise geometries that align with natural growth patterns, spirals, hexagons, and golden ratios.

Biologist Jeremy Narby, in his book The Cosmic Serpent, proposed that some ancient cultures may have intuitively understood the double-helix structure of DNA long before its scientific discovery. Symbols like the Caduceus, the Ouroboros, and the Chakra system seem to mirror patterns seen in molecular biology, raising questions about whether these symbols emerged from a deeper subconscious awareness of biological coding.

While modern science has yet to confirm how symbols might directly alter DNA expression, their psychological influence is undeniable. Symbols evoke powerful mental states , calmness, focus, or empowerment which in turn can trigger hormonal and neurological shifts capable of influencing genetic behavior.

The Future of Art and Biology

Art has always been more than expression—it's communication. But perhaps that communication goes deeper than we once believed, reaching into the very language of our cells. Whether through visual patterns, sound vibrations, or physical movement, art may carry forgotten keys to unlocking our biological potential.

In blending ancient practices with modern science, we may rediscover what the mystics knew all along, *"art doesn't just reflect who we are; it has the power to shape what we become."*If DNA is the ultimate art form-alive, evolving, and interactive then art itself may be a forgotten language for reprogramming the self.

While researching this, I came across a passage from Siddhartha Mukherjee's The Gene: An Intimate History that struck me: *"Genes are like stories, endlessly rewritten, whispered down through generations—not fixed commands, but shifting instructions waiting to be shaped by experience."*

CHAPTER TEN

AETHER

(The Art of the Cosmos)

"When the universe paints with stars and mathematics."

Are Aliens Truly Alien?

For centuries, we have looked up at the stars and wondered, Are we alone? But what if the question itself is flawed? What if extraterrestrials are not strange, robotic beings from distant galaxies, but rather, civilizations parallel to our own , hidden not by distance, but by perception?

As Liu Cixin writes, this idea comes from The Three-Body Problem ,

"The universe is a dark forest. Every civilization is an armed hunter, stalking through the trees like a ghost, gently pushing aside branches that block the path and trying to tread without sound. Even breathing must be done with care, because in the forest, there are others—hunters like you. If you find another life, another hunter, there's only one thing you can do: eliminate it."

The way we define "alien" is a limitation of human understanding. We assume that if life exists elsewhere, it must follow the biological and technological patterns we recognize. But what if life is already here, just beyond the veil of our perception? What if the true civilizations of the cosmos have always existed, not in distant solar systems, but in spaces we cannot yet access—hidden dimensions, parallel worlds, or even unseen realms on planets we have already "explored"?

I am not saying that life in other worlds does not exist. What I mean to say is , what if there is also a possibility of this? We never see reality as it truly is; our eyes are not capable of perceiving everything. Just as there are spectrums of light and sound beyond human senses, could there also be forms of life, civilizations, or even entire ecosystems existing outside our current perception? Perhaps what we call "alien" is not distant, but merely unseen.

The Moon: A Case of Selective Perception?

Consider our own Moon , one of the most mysterious celestial bodies in human history. It orbits us with an strange precision, its far side never visible from Earth. Every time we send probes or astronauts, they land in predictable, chosen locations. But what if the real secrets of the Moon are deliberately kept from us?

Ancient texts across cultures speak of the Moon as more than just a celestial body; some describe it as a gateway, a watchtower, or even an artificial construct. The idea sounds fantastical, but let's explore the possibilities,

{ Hidden Lunar Civilizations }

What if there exists a thriving ecosystem on the Moon, not visible to us because we lack the sensory capability to perceive it? Just as infrared and ultraviolet light were once invisible to human eyes until we developed technology to detect them, could there be entire spectra of existence on the Moon we are blind to?

The Moon has always been more than just a celestial body, it has been a symbol, a mystery, a presence woven into the myths and sacred texts of ancient civilizations. In the vast expanse of human history, cultures from India to Sumer, from Greece to Mesoamerica, did not merely see the Moon as a lifeless rock in the sky. They spoke of it as a realm, a kingdom, a sanctuary of gods and unknown forces.

Hindu scriptures describe Chandra Loka, the Moon Realm, as a celestial plane where enlightened souls rest before their next incarnation. In the Vishnu Purana, the Moon is not merely an orbiting body but a world brimming with divine energy, deeply connected to the cosmic order. The Rig Veda speaks of Soma, a mystical elixir of immortality, closely linked to the Moon's essence. Beyond poetic symbolism, ancient knowledge preserved in these texts suggests that the Moon was understood as a source of energy, a gateway, or even a place of higher consciousness.

In Sumerian and Babylonian records, the Moon was the throne of Sin (Nanna), the great lunar deity, ruling over celestial domains. The Sumerians, among the first astronomers, documented cosmic events with precision, describing the Moon not just as an object of study but as an entity intertwined with divine intelligence. Their records hold accounts of celestial battles and the presence of unknown forces, hinting at a perspective far removed from the modern, reduced view of the Moon as barren and lifeless.

Plutarch, in On the Face in the Moon, examined the Moon's nature, considering it more than a mere rock in space. The Pythagoreans, seekers of hidden truths, spoke of counter-Earths and celestial bodies beyond human perception, including the Moon as a possible domain of unseen existence. In Mesoamerican traditions, the Moon was revered not only for its cycles but for its influence over fate, civilization, and spiritual forces, guarded by priests who interpreted its movements with absolute precision.

The ancients did not speak of a cold, barren world, they saw something else, something alive, something hidden. What if they were right?

{Directed Exploration}

The Moon has been a site of curiosity, myth, and controlled access for centuries. Every modern lunar mission lands on the same familiar regions, carefully mapped and deemed "safe." But why is it that the far side of the Moon, the one never visible from Earth , remains largely unexplored, its mysteries left untouched?

If intelligence beyond our own exists, then directed exploration is not merely a strategy but a necessity. What if the very nature of space exploration is being guided , not just by agencies and governments, but by forces beyond human authority? Ancient texts across civilizations reference celestial beings residing on or beyond the Moon, describing it not as a barren rock but as a domain of hidden knowledge. The Vimanas of Indian epics, the Watcher Angels of Abrahamic traditions, and the enigmatic lunar deities of Mesopotamia all suggest a history that predates modern exploration.

Today, technology allows us to observe exoplanets light-years away, yet our closest cosmic neighbor remains a place of calculated restriction. The idea of space agencies curating information is not new, but if there is something to conceal, the true control may not be in human hands. What if our access to the Moon is permitted only within certain boundaries, and what lies beyond is something we are not meant or not ready to see?

{The Moon as an Observation Post }

The Moon is more than Earth's silent companion—it is an anomaly. Its perfect positioning, unnaturally large size relative to the planet, and locked orbit that ensures only one side is ever visible defy conventional celestial mechanics. Such precise conditions are unlikely to be the result of mere chance. Some physicists and researchers propose that the Moon's placement suggests deliberate positioning, hinting at an intelligence beyond known history.

Scientific missions have detected unexplained seismic activity on the Moon, suggesting a hollow or partially artificial interior. Unusual electromagnetic disturbances and regions of unexpected heat emission further support the notion that the Moon is not just a lifeless rock. The control over what is studied and revealed about the Moon has always been selective, with certain anomalies left unexplored or dismissed. Modern instruments are designed to detect expected geological formations, yet the true evidence may lie in structures, signals, or materials beyond current comprehension. If remnants of an ancient intelligence exist on the Moon, their recognition requires breaking free from the limitations of conventional science.

Ancient Civilizations and Their Connection to the 'Aliens'

If we turn to ancient knowledge, we find something striking, the so called "gods" of past civilizations were not passive deities but engineers, architects, and scientists. They built structures that defy modern replication. They spoke of cosmic visitors and higher realms, of knowledge that was "given" to them by forces beyond human comprehension.

But what if these gods were not mythical at all? What if they were in contact with non-human intelligence and beings we today would call "aliens," but who might have simply been life forms from higher dimensions or parallel worlds?

Clues from Ancient Structures

The Pyramids of Egypt and Mesoamerica - The mathematical precision of these structures, their alignment with celestial bodies, and their energetic properties suggest an understanding of science far beyond what we credit ancient civilizations with. What if these pyramids were not tombs, but receivers, devices that allowed communication or even transportation across cosmic distances?

Vimanas of Ancient India - Described in the Vedas, these flying crafts were said to be piloted by beings with knowledge of celestial navigation, gravitational forces, and energy fields. Could these descriptions be records of ancient technological contact rather than mythology?

Megalithic Temples and Cosmic Tuning Forks - Structures like Göbekli Tepe, Stonehenge, and the temples of Puma Punku resonate with specific frequencies. Were these places of communication with extraterrestrial intelligences, places where human minds could be expanded, where information could be received?

If the ancients had access to knowledge far beyond our current scientific grasp, where did it go? Over time, whether through lost manuscripts, erased histories, or shifts in human consciousness, this connection faded, leaving behind only fragments of a once-greater understanding.

Are We Trapped in a Limited Perception of Reality?

Modern science is built on observation. But what if observation itself is flawed?

Imagine standing in a room with a single window. Everything you know about the world outside is based on what you can see through that frame. Now, what if the real world is not just outside the window, but all around you hidden in frequencies your eyes cannot detect?

Ancient wisdom tells us that reality is multi-layered, that there are dimensions of existence beyond what the five senses perceive. According to mordern physics ,

Quantum Mechanics and the Multiverse Theory- The notion that multiple realities can exist simultaneously aligns eerily with ancient texts that speak of multiple realms of existence.

Dark Matter and Energy- Scientists now believe that 95% of the universe is made up of "dark" material, something we cannot see, touch, or interact with. What if that 95% contains civilizations, life forms, and knowledge beyond our current reach?

The Simulation Hypothesis: If reality is a programmed construct, as some physicists propose, then it stands to reason that those who programmed it , whether natural cosmic forces or advanced beings, might be able to modify it, and perhaps communicate with those who understand its code.

What This Means for Our Future

If ancient civilizations were communicating with these intelligences, can we do the same? And if so, how?

Reawakening Ancient Knowledge: Modern science is rediscovering what the ancients already knew that is frequency, vibration, and energy fields play a critical role in unlocking higher understanding. The more we study the structures, texts, and technologies of the past, the closer we may come to reopening these channels of knowledge.

Expanding Human Perception: Just as technology allowed us to see X-rays and radio waves, we may need new tools or new forms of consciousness to perceive what lies beyond our reality frame. Meditation, frequency tuning, and altered states of awareness have been used for centuries to access hidden knowledge.

Challenging the Narrative: If our current perception of extraterrestrial life is based on Hollywood-inspired robotic creatures, it is time to reconsider. The "aliens" may not be distant visitors, but entities that have been interacting with us since the beginning guiding civilizations, shaping knowledge, and perhaps waiting for us to reclaim what we have forgotten.

Final Thought: Who Are the Real Aliens?

If we are disconnected from the knowledge that once built civilizations, if we have lost the ability to see beyond our narrow perception, if we ignore the ancient signals that still resonate in forgotten temples and cosmic alignments—*then perhaps we are the real aliens*. Perhaps we are the ones who have become foreign to the deeper truths of existence.

The cosmos is not silent. *BE READY TO LISTEN* .

“*"Not only is the universe stranger than we imagine, it is stranger than we can imagine." — Arthur Eddington*”

The Music of the Planets

> *"At depth on Jupiter and Saturn, the pressures are so great that atoms sweat electrons, and the air becomes a metal."*

The universe is not silent, *it sings*. Its melodies are hidden within the fabric of space-time, vibrating at frequencies beyond human perception. Among all celestial bodies, Saturn stands out as an enigma, not just in its physical grandeur but in its deep connection to ancient knowledge, human consciousness, and the cosmic order. Its rings, a celestial orchestra of frozen matter, produce a hum , a soundless frequency that holds secrets yet to be fully deciphered.

But why is Saturn so important to us?

Why Saturn? A Cosmic Key to Human Understanding

Saturn has fascinated civilizations for millennia, not just as a planet but as a symbol of time, wisdom, and hidden knowledge. Across cultures, it has been associated with divine intelligence, alchemy, and even human destiny. Could its planetary resonance hold deeper secrets about our consciousness and evolution?

Here are a few intriguing reasons why Saturn remains central to both scientific discovery and ancient mysticism,

[The Architect of Time and Reality]

In Roman mythology, Saturn was the god of time (Chronos in Greek). This association with time aligns with *modern physics*, where Saturn's massive gravitational pull affects the space-time fabric around it. Some even theorize that Saturn's rings hold a vibrational key to time distortion. Saturn completes an orbit around the Sun roughly every 29.5 years, a cycle that correlates with major turning points in human life, known as the Saturn Return in astrology as periods of transformation, challenges, and awakening.

[The Planet of Frequencies and Vibration]

The rings of Saturn are composed of billions of ice and rock particles that create resonance structures which are mathematical formations that mirror the harmonic scales found in music. NASA's Cassini spacecraft detected that Saturn's rings generate electromagnetic waves that interact with the planet's magnetic field, producing frequencies far beyond human hearing.

[A Connection to Ancient Civilizations]

Many ancient societies, including the Babylonians, Egyptians, and Hindus, revered Saturn as the *guardian of hidden wisdom*. Some occult traditions even suggest that Saturn's vibrational influence shaped early human consciousness. *The Hexagon Storm at Saturn's north pole,* a massive, perfectly geometric storm that has puzzled scientists. Some esoteric thinkers propose that this hexagonal structure is a natural portal or a cosmic tuning device that affects Earth's frequency.

Here are some casebased studies ,

The Saturnian Influence on Human Consciousness

One of the most mysterious aspects of the Great Pyramid of Giza is its resonance. Researchers have found that the King's Chamber within the pyramid resonates at a frequency close to 7.83 Hz, which matches Earth's Schumann resonance (the natural electromagnetic frequency of our planet). Interestingly, some

Saturnian frequencies also align with this range. Could it be that the builders of the pyramids were tuning into planetary harmonics, possibly including those of Saturn? Some speculate that the pyramids were not just tombs but energy amplifiers that connected to celestial bodies like Saturn, absorbing and redistributing vibrational knowledge.

NASA's Cassini Discoveries – The Sound of Saturn's Rings

In 2017, NASA's Cassini mission recorded plasma waves traveling between Saturn and its moon, Enceladus. These plasma waves, when converted into audio, produced a haunting, rhythmic sound , almost like a deep-space heartbeat. What does this mean? Plasma waves function similarly to sound waves, except they travel through space's charged particles. The rhythmic nature suggests that Saturn's rings are not random structures but are interacting with the planet's magnetic field in an organized, almost musical way.

The sound pattern is similar to the patterns found in human brainwaves, could there be an unknown connection between Saturn's frequencies and consciousness? NASA's research into these frequencies is still ongoing, but one theory suggests that celestial bodies, especially ones with rings like Saturn, might act as cosmic broadcasters, sending out information in vibrational form.

Saturn's Connection to Crop Circles and Geometric Codes

Some of the most intricate crop circles ever recorded have had direct correlations to Saturn's geometry. In 1996, a crop circle in England was found to resemble the exact hexagonal storm pattern on Saturn's north pole. Other formations have mirrored the orbital ratios of Saturn's moons. Some researchers believe that these geometric patterns could be messages encoded in frequency, possibly even transmitted through Saturn's vibrational field.

This leads to an even bigger question, are celestial bodies like Saturn communicating in ways we have yet to understand?

Can Saturn's Vibrations Be Used for Human Advancement?

If Saturn emits frequencies that align with human consciousness, we possibly can harness these vibrations for science, healing, or even interstellar communication.

[Healing Through Planetary Frequencies]

Sound therapy already shows that certain frequencies can alter brain states. If Saturn's waves match human brainwave activity, could they be used for deep meditation or cognitive enhancement? Some monks use Tibetan singing bowls, which create frequencies that resemble planetary resonance. This could be an ancient technique of attuning to cosmic sounds.

[Time Manipulation and Consciousness Shifts]

Some quantum physicists suggest that frequencies and vibrations can affect perceptions of time. Saturn, as the planet of time (Chronos), might hold keys to understanding this relationship. Perhaps exposure to Saturn's vibrational patterns can alter our perception of time and reality.

[Interplanetary Communication]

If Saturn is generating structured waves, it is possible that they are carrying information, perhaps even signals from extraterrestrial intelligence. Ancient civilizations might have understood how to receive and decode these messages. Modern technology, such as radio telescopes, is only now catching up to what may have been known thousands of years ago.

Final Thoughts: Are We Finally Listening?

For centuries, Saturn has been depicted as a gatekeeper of cosmic knowledge, a planet whose rings sing in silent frequencies. With modern science validating ancient beliefs, we stand at the edge of a profound realization, The universe is not random; it is structured through vibration and frequency. Saturn's rings produce real sound waves that interact with consciousness. Ancient civilizations may have tuned into these frequencies for wisdom, healing, and possibly even extraterrestrial communication.Perhaps the reason we are only now beginning to hear Saturn's symphony is that we are finally ready to listen.

The Frequencies of Other Planets

Every Planet Has a Song—Decoding the Cosmic Orchestra

If Saturn's rings hum in inaudible frequencies, what about the other planets? Does each celestial body have its own vibrational signature, a unique resonance that influences the universe ?

Science confirms that planets do, in fact, emit their own electromagnetic frequencies, often through interactions with the solar wind, magnetic fields, or even their moons. NASA's space probes, Voyager, Cassini, and Juno have captured these cosmic actions, revealing a fascinating truth, each planet "sings," broadcasting signals across space in frequencies beyond human perception.

But beyond the scientific data, could these planetary frequencies influence human consciousness, evolution, or even the very fabric of reality itself?

Planetary Frequencies: A Scientific and Esoteric Breakdown

1. *Mercury – The Whisper of the Messenger*

Scientific Insight: Mercury, the closest planet to the Sun, interacts strongly with solar wind, creating rapid bursts of electromagnetic waves. NASA's MESSENGER spacecraft detected high-frequency radio waves caused by charged particles moving through its weak magnetic field.

Esoteric Connection: In mythology, Mercury (Hermes in Greek) is the messenger of the gods. Its high-frequency emissions may symbolize quick transmission of knowledge, thought, and intelligence. Could it be that Mercury's vibrational nature aligns with the mind's ability to process and send information rapidly?

2. *Venus – The Harmonic Pulse of Love and Chaos*

Scientific Insight: Venus, often called Earth's twin, produces a deep, pulsating sound recorded by NASA's Parker Solar Probe. This is due to interactions between its thick atmosphere and solar radiation, generating low-frequency plasma waves.

Esoteric Connection: Venus is associated with love, beauty, and harmony in mythology, yet its surface is a hellish landscape of extreme temperatures and acidic storms. This duality mirrors the way frequencies can either harmonize or destroy. Could Venusian frequencies hold the key to balancing extreme forces, both in nature and human emotions?

3. *Earth – The Schumann Resonance and the Pulse of Life*

Scientific Insight: Earth's Schumann resonance vibrates at 7.83 Hz, a frequency that directly affects human brainwaves and is linked to states of deep relaxation and intuition. This electromagnetic pulse is created by lightning discharges in the ionosphere.

Esoteric Connection: Ancient spiritual traditions believed Earth itself was alive, vibrating in tune with human consciousness. Many meditation practices aim to align with the Schumann resonance, suggesting that planetary frequencies can be harnessed for mental and physical well-being.

4. *Mars – The Echo of a Lost Civilization?*

Scientific Insight: Mars produces low-frequency vibrations, with NASA's InSight lander detecting unusual seismic waves (marsquakes) that create deep, rumbling tones. Its thin atmosphere also allows wind-driven acoustic waves to travel differently than on Earth.

Esoteric Connection: Many ancient texts speak of Mars as a planet of war and destruction, yet recent theories suggest Mars may have once hosted advanced life. Some researchers speculate that the low-frequency waves of Mars might contain information embedded within them, remnants of a lost era.

5. Jupiter – The Deep Roar of the King

Scientific Insight: Jupiter's massive magnetic field generates some of the loudest electromagnetic waves in the solar system. NASA's Juno spacecraft recorded intense radio bursts and plasma wave oscillations coming from its poles.

Esoteric Connection: In mythology, Jupiter (Zeus) is the ruler of the gods. In astrology, it represents expansion, wisdom, and power. The planet's deep, resonant frequencies could be seen as the cosmic "voice of authority," influencing large-scale shifts in consciousness and destiny. Some even suggest that Jupiter's frequencies help maintain the electromagnetic balance of the solar system.

6. Saturn – The Cosmic Tuner (Revisited)

Scientific Insight: Saturn's rings produce structured, musical plasma waves that interact with the planet's magnetic field. This organized resonance suggests a mathematical precision akin to a cosmic tuning fork.

Esoteric Connection: As previously discussed, Saturn has long been seen as the gatekeeper of time and hidden knowledge. Its frequencies might act as a tuning mechanism, influencing planetary and possibly human evolution.

7. Uranus – The Mysterious Whisperer

Scientific Insight: Uranus is unique, it emits odd, fluctuating radio signals that scientists still struggle to explain. These pulses are chaotic and don't follow the same rhythmic patterns as other planets.

Esoteric Connection: Uranus is associated with revolution and sudden change. Its erratic frequencies might symbolize the breaking of old structures, pushing humanity toward new paradigms of thought.

8. Neptune – The Mystic's Song

Scientific Insight: Neptune's frequencies are deep, slow, and rhythmic, resembling ocean waves. This is due to the planet's thick atmosphere interacting with magnetic field disturbances.

Esoteric Connection: Neptune is linked to dreams, intuition, and the subconscious. Some claim that meditating on Neptune's frequencies can help access deeper levels of consciousness and forgotten knowledge.

9. Pluto – The Silent Frequency of the Underworld

Scientific Insight: Though Pluto is small, it still emits weak electromagnetic pulses. However, due to its distance, its signals are faint and difficult to detect.

Esoteric Connection: Pluto is associated with transformation, death, and rebirth. Its nearly undetectable hum could symbolize hidden truths, energies that exist beyond normal perception.

Are We Missing Something? The Potential of Planetary Harmonics

Ancient knowledge and modern science suggest that planetary frequencies might be more than just random cosmic noise. Here's why this matters, Scientists have found that sound frequencies can alter DNA expression. Some researchers suggest that listening to planetary frequencies (converted to human-audible sounds) can induce altered states of consciousness. Tibetan monks and ancient mystics may have attuned their minds to these frequencies through chanting and meditative practices.

Final Thoughts: Are We in Tune with the Cosmic Symphony?

The more we study planetary frequencies, the more we realize that the *universe operates like a vast musical composition*. Each planet contributes its own note to the grand cosmic orchestra. But here's the real question: Are we, as humans, attuned to this music? If we could decode these frequencies fully, could we unlock hidden aspects of our consciousness?Could planetary harmonics hold the key to interstellar knowledge, healing, or even time travel?

For scientists, understanding planetary frequencies could deepen research into bioelectromagnetism, neurobiology, and even the possibility of interstellar communication. Some physicists theorize that these frequencies might reveal patterns in spacetime or act as cosmic markers for advanced civilizations. Artists, on the other hand, have long sought inspiration from celestial harmonies, Johannes Kepler's *Harmonices Mundi* (1619) proposed that planets move in musical ratios, suggesting that the universe itself is an orchestration of sound.

Because whether you acknowledge it or not, you are already part of these frequencies. Every cell in your body, every thought in your mind, vibrates at a frequency that interacts with the universe. Ignoring this doesn't make it irrelevant , it only leaves you unaware of the forces shaping your existence.

Think about it. The same gravitational pull that locks planets in orbit also holds your feet to the ground. The same electromagnetic forces that ripple through Saturn's rings pulse through your nervous system. If scientists are decoding the hidden symphony of planetary frequencies and artists are turning them into music, what does that tell us? That reality itself is built on vibrations.

If you learn to tune in, to listen, to resonate, to align then you don't just hear the universe. You become part of its rhythm. You start living in sync with something greater, something ancient, something that has always been there, waiting for you to remember.

The Cosmic Canvas: Nebulae

When we gaze at images of nebulae, vast, colorful clouds of gas and dust, we are seeing the universe at its most artistic. Swirling hues of deep blues, fiery reds, and ethereal purples stretch across the cosmos, as if an unseen hand has painted the void. But are nebulae just cosmic accidents, or is there a deeper intelligence at play?

The Universe as an Artist

If we consider creation as a form of art, nebulae are the universe's unfinished masterpieces. Every nebula is a dynamic structure, shifting and evolving over thousands or even millions of years. The colors we see are not random, they emerge from the physics of ionization, where gases absorb and re-emit light at different wavelengths. But why do they take on such stunning forms? Some resemble flowers, others vast wings, dragons, or eyes. Is this simply our brains imposing patterns (pareidolia), or is there a deeper structure ?

What Are Nebulae? A nebula (Latin for "cloud") is a colossal cloud of gas and dust floating in interstellar space. They come in several types. Emission Nebulae – Glow brightly as their gases are energized by nearby stars (e.g., Orion Nebula). Reflection Nebulae – Reflect the light of stars, often appearing blue due to scattering (e.g., Witch Head Nebula). Dark Nebulae – Opaque clouds blocking background light (e.g., Horsehead Nebula). Planetary Nebulae – The remnants of dying stars, forming delicate, colorful rings (e.g., Helix Nebula). Supernova Remnants – The explosive remains of stars (e.g., Crab Nebula).

Each nebula is a different kind of brushstroke in the vast mural of the universe, each a unique expression of stellar life and death.

The Language of Color in Space

Just like a painter selects colors to evoke emotions, the universe uses specific elements to craft its glowing wonders. Red – Hydrogen, the most abundant element in the cosmos, glows red when ionized. Blue – Reflection nebulae glow blue due to Rayleigh scattering, the same reason Earth's sky is blue. Green – Oxygen, found in planetary nebulae, glows an eerie green. Yellow & Orange – Sulfur and other heavy elements create warm tones in nebulae.

Could these colors contain hidden messages? Ancient civilizations often linked colors to higher knowledge, red with creation, blue with divinity, green with life. Perhaps nebulae channel cosmic secrets through their hues.

Are Nebulae Conscious?

This is where science meets philosophy. Some physicists propose that the universe itself is conscious, a self-aware entity unfolding across time. If this is true, then nebulae could be more than just celestial clouds, they could be cosmic thoughts taking form.

In Hindu cosmology, creation emerges from divine sound (Nada Brahma), and nebulae could be echoes of the universe's first breath. In Kabbalah, the Tree of Life describes stages of creation, mirroring how nebulae birth stars that eventually give rise to planets. Some modern theories suggest nebulae are like neural networks, spreading filaments of gas in ways that resemble brain synapses. Is it possible that the universe itself be thinking ?

The Orion Nebula – A Cosmic Womb

The Orion Nebula (M42) is a huge cloud of glowing gas and dust, stretching across 24 light-years. It is not just a beautiful sight in the night sky, it is a place where new stars are born. This vast cosmic nursery contains the basic building blocks that form planets, moons, and even the elements needed for life. Located in the sword of the Orion constellation, it is the closest large star-forming region to Earth, about 1,344 light-years away. It gives us a rare glimpse into how stars and planetary systems come into existence.

At its heart is the Trapezium Cluster, a group of bright young stars that release strong ultraviolet radiation, causing the surrounding gas to glow. This glowing effect helps us see the process of creation and destruction, where clouds of dust collapse to form new stars while powerful stellar winds shape the nebula. The Orion Nebula is a place of change, where cosmic dust transforms into structured systems, showing us the endless cycle of birth and rebirth in the universe.

Nebulae as Portals – The Ancient Perspective

Ancient civilizations saw something more in Orion. To the Egyptians, the Orion constellation was linked to Osiris, the god of resurrection, and they believed the souls of pharaohs traveled to Orion after death. The Maya associated Orion with creation itself, and the Hopi of North America considered it a gateway between worlds. Could these myths have a foundation in something real, something science is only now beginning to understand?

Quantum physics and modern cosmology hint at the possibility that nebulae, with their vast energy fields and extreme gravitational forces, could act as more than just stellar nurseries. Some researchers speculate that the intense energy fluctuations and high-density plasma within these regions could affect space-time in ways we can't understand now . The concept of "cosmic tunnels" or Einstein-Rosen bridges, commonly known as wormholes, suggests that highly energetic zones like nebulae might have the potential to bend or connect distant points in space-time.

While mainstream astrophysics does not yet support the idea of nebulae as literal portals, they undeniably represent a threshold, the transition from diffuse cosmic dust to structured stellar systems. Whether these formations serve as physical gateways or merely as metaphors for transformation, their significance remains profound. They are cosmic paintings in motion, shaping the evolution of the universe itself.

The Orion Nebula, a masterpiece still in progress, continues to challenge the boundaries of what we know—and what we dream is possible.

Nebulae and the Role of Ancient Art

Ancient civilizations created artworks with swirling patterns that look surprisingly similar to nebulae. These patterns appear in rock carvings, mandalas, and temple designs, long before telescopes existed to reveal the true forms of nebulae. This raises an interesting possibility: how did early people know about these cosmic structures?

One idea is that they saw them in visions or altered states of mind. Many ancient cultures practiced meditation, rituals, and even used special plants to experience spiritual journeys. Shamans and sages often spoke of traveling to glowing, swirling realms, descriptions that sound much like modern images of nebulae. Some traditions, like the Vedic idea of the "Akashic Records," suggest that all knowledge exists in a universal energy field, which might explain how ancient people gained insight into things beyond their time.

Another theory is that they were guided by advanced beings. Many ancient stories describe gods or visitors from the sky who brought wisdom and shaped human understanding of the universe. Some believe these beings could have shared knowledge about space, leaving behind symbols and carvings that we now recognize as nebula-like patterns. Perhaps the "Aliens" we discussed earlier .

It invites us to reconsider the nature of human perception and our place in the vast, unfolding tapestry of the universe.

Conclusion: The Universe as a Living Artwork

Nebulae are not just random gas clouds; they are the blueprints of cosmic evolution. They give birth to stars, shape galaxies, and provide the raw material for planets—*perhaps even life.* If we view the universe as an artist, nebulae are the strokes of its infinite imagination.

But beyond science, there remains a mystery. Are these cosmic paintings revealing something deeper? Are they mere beauty, or are they encoded messages from the cosmos itself?

Likely in understanding nebulae, *we are learning to read the universe's own handwriting. Reaveling us the knowledge to be the greatest.*

CHAPTER ELEVEN

SECRETUM

(The Alchemist's Final Secret)

The Illusion of Separation

For centuries, knowledge has been carefully divided, placed into separate compartments as if each subject existed in isolation. Science is seen as the realm of reason, logic, and numbers, while art is seen as boundless expression, intuition, and creativity. The modern mind has been conditioned to believe in these separations, but *what if this division is the greatest deception of all?*

The alchemists, those ancient seekers of transformation, understood something we have lost, *the unity of all things*. They did not see chemistry as separate from philosophy, nor astronomy as separate from poetry. They worked in secret, encrypting their wisdom in symbols and allegories, hinting at a truth too powerful for a world obsessed with compartmentalization. That truth? *"Art and science are not separate—they are the same force, wearing different masks."*

> "*The Hermetic Principle of Polarity, often phrased as "Opposites are equal in nature, but different in degree,"*"

If this is true, then what else have we been misled about?

THE GRAND ILLUSION

To see the world as it truly is, one must first recognize the veil that has been pulled over our eyes. This illusion is so deeply ingrained that it feels natural, unquestionable—yet, *it is an illusion* nonetheless. It tells us that structure and creativity are opposing forces when, in reality, they are interwoven threads of the same cosmic fabric.

Consider the Renaissance, an era that birthed some of the most brilliant minds in human history. Leonardo da Vinci was not just a painter but an anatomist, engineer, and scientist. He saw no distinction between his sketches of the human body and his designs for flying machines because he understood that all knowledge flows from the same source. Nikola Tesla, often called the man who saw the future, did not invent in isolation, he drew inspiration from the harmony of the universe, speaking of energy, vibration, and frequency as the very essence of reality.

The ancients knew this well. To them, the stars were not just distant fires; they were stories, energies, and forces that shaped reality. The pyramids were not just tombs but structures embedded with mathematical precision, designed to interact with the cosmos in ways we still fail to comprehend. Even music was never just entertainment, it was a force that resonated with the very fabric of existence, a tool for healing, transformation, and even *communication with realms* beyond our perception.

But somewhere along the way, this knowledge was fragmented, divided, and diluted. The alchemists wrote their wisdom in codes because they knew society was not ready to see beyond the illusion. And perhaps, we are still struggling to wake up.

THE ALCHEMICAL THREAD THAT CONNECTS ALL THINGS

If we follow the thread of ancient wisdom, we begin to see a pattern. *Every true genius in history, every revolutionary thinker, possessed the ability to see the unity of all things.*

When we look at the cosmos, we see an infinite expanse of swirling galaxies, nebulae stretching like brushstrokes across the blackness of space. The universe is a painting in motion, a grand symphony of creation. But if we view it only through the lens of science, reducing it to equations and calculations, we miss its essence. Likewise, if we see it only as an abstract mystery without seeking to understand its mechanisms, we remain blind. It is only by merging these perspectives that we glimpse the truth.

Take Saturn, for instance, a planet that has fascinated mystics and scientists alike. Its rings emit frequencies we cannot hear, yet these frequencies exist, vibrating in dimensions just beyond our perception. Is this not like music, a melody too vast and subtle for human ears? And what of the countless cultures that revered Saturn, associating it with time, wisdom, and hidden knowledge? They did not create these associations without reason, nor did these symbols and stories emerge from nowhere. Either they sensed something we have long forgotten, or their understanding was rooted in a deeper truth, one that modern science has yet to fully grasp.

Ancient texts speak of the harmony of the spheres, the idea that planets produce music as they move through space. Kepler, the astronomer who gave us the laws of planetary motion, did not view the cosmos as a cold, mechanical system, he described it as a divine composition, where each celestial body plays a note in a grand orchestra. To him, *numbers were not sterile figures but the rhythm of the universe itself.*

And here lies the secret that has been buried: ***Science and art are one*** because the universe itself is both mathematical and poetic. It is an endless dance of structure and spontaneity, precision and fluidity. The ancients understood this. The greatest minds of history rediscovered it. And now, we must remember.

THE LOST CONNECTION TO ANCIENT KNOWLEDGE

What if the secrets of the universe were already known, long before modern science, and we have simply forgotten? The pyramids of Egypt encode precise astronomical knowledge, aligning with the stars in ways that should have been impossible for an ancient civilization. The Mayans tracked cosmic cycles with astonishing accuracy, predicting celestial events thousands of years into the future. The Vedic texts of India speak of cosmic vibrations, mantras that align the human mind with the frequencies of the universe. And yet, today, we dismiss these ancient insights as mere myth, while struggling to comprehend the very same truths through scientific means.

But what if these civilizations were not separate from what we now call science? What if their knowledge came from a different kind of understanding, one that did not divide the world into categories, but saw it as a seamless whole. Alchemy was never just about turning lead into gold. It was about transmutation, of matter, of the mind, of the soul. The "gold" the alchemists sought was not physical wealth but enlightenment, the unification of all knowledge into a single, radiant truth.

And this truth remains as disregarded now as it was then. Once, knowledge was the privilege of the few, the sages, the mystics, the architects of understanding while the rest were kept in the dark. Today, information is abundant, yet true wisdom is suffocated beneath a veil of illusion. Ignorance is no longer imposed; it is embraced, shaped by the voices of fthe decieved who do not seek truth but command obedience.

WHAT ELSE HAVE WE BEEN DECEIVED ABOUT?

If art and science are not separate, then what other false divisions have shaped our understanding?

We have been told that reason and intuition are opposites. In reality, they are two sides of the same process—discovery. We have been taught that the ancients were primitive. Yet their structures, knowledge, and philosophies still baffle modern scholars. We have been conditioned to see the universe as mechanical. But it behaves like an artist's masterpiece, filled with hidden harmonies and intricate design. We have been led to believe that consciousness is a byproduct of biology. But what if it is something greater,something coded into the structure of reality itself?

The greatest deception is the illusion of separation. And the greatest awakening is the realization that everything is connected.

THE ALCHEMIST'S FINAL SECRET

The alchemists hid their wisdom because they knew that most people were not ready to see beyond the illusion. But the time has come to remember. If art and science are one, then the universe is both a painting and an equation, a symphony and a formula. The cosmos does not operate in parts, it is a masterpiece of unity. *This is the secret* that da Vinci, Tesla, and the ancient sages understood. This is the wisdom encoded in forgotten texts, whispered through the stars, resonating in the very fabric of our existence.

And this is the knowledge that, once rediscovered, will change everything.

Existence- a Form of Divine Design?

Everything we know, everything we see, hear, touch, every experience we've ever had, has been filtered through the limits of human perception. And yet, if we strip away our personal biases, if we look at the fundamental nature of reality, something remarkable emerges: *the universe is not chaos*. It is not an accident.

Everywhere, across time, across disciplines, a pattern reveals itself. In science, in art, in music, in ancient wisdom—*there is a code*, a structure, a rhythm to existence. Some call it mathematics, some call it sacred geometry, some call it divine intelligence. But at its core, it asks a simple, haunting question, *Is reality designed?* And if so, by whom or by what?

The Language of the Universe: Mathematics or Mysticism?

There was a time when science and mysticism were not at war. The greatest minds of history, Pythagoras, Da Vinci, Kepler, Newton saw no separation between numbers and the divine, between equations and art. To them, the universe was a vast, living manuscript, written in mathematical perfection. But was mathematics something humans created to describe reality? Perhaps it was the very foundation of reality itself.

Take the Fibonacci sequence,an infinite pattern that appears in the spirals of galaxies, the unfurling of ferns, the symmetry of seashells. It is not random; it is embedded in nature itself. Or consider the Golden Ratio, the proportion that artists and architects have used for centuries, believing it to be the key to perfect beauty. It is found in the Parthenon, in the Mona Lisa, in the human face itself.

Is this simply how physics works, or is it evidence of an intelligence beyond our comprehension?

The Illusion of Chaos: Why Reality is Not What it Seems

Science tells us that everything is made of atoms—tiny particles that form the physical world. But what if those atoms are not solid, not even "real" in the way we understand reality? At the quantum level, particles do not exist in a definite state until they are observed. Reality, in its most fundamental form, is shaped by perception.

This is not a mystical belief. This is physics.

The famous double-slit experiment showed that light behaves both as a particle and a wave, until it is measured. Once observed, it chooses a definite form, as if consciousness itself determines reality. If that is true, then what we see, what we touch, what we experience is not an objective universe, but something fluid, something interactive.

If ancient wisdom had spoken of a great illusion, calling it Maya, were they describing this very phenomenon? That what we believe to be solid, permanent, and external... is in fact shifting, responding, perhaps even designed. And if we truly understand this illusion *then we can create our own illusion* , i remember hearing this for the first time from the mysterious man.

The Architect or the Algorithm?

If the universe is not random, if reality follows precise, measurable patterns, then the next question follows naturally, who—or what—designed it? There are two ways to approach this question.

One is the spiritual path, the belief that an intelligence beyond our understanding created the cosmos, shaping it with numbers, energy, and consciousness. That what we call "God" or "Source" or the "Universal Mind" is not separate from existence, but woven into its very essence.

The other is the computational path, the theory that we live in a simulation, a vast, coded reality running on laws of physics we are only beginning to decode. Some of the greatest minds in science, Elon Musk, Nick Bostrom, even physicist James Gates have suggested that at the deepest levels of reality, we find what appears to be computer code.

Could it be that existence itself is a form of hyper-advanced simulation? That what we call divine patterns are actually the mathematical fingerprints of an unfathomably advanced intelligence? Quite possibly they are merely the same idea in different languages. Perhaps even both .

The Holographic Universe and the Hermetic Mirror

Another stunning revelation in modern physics is the Holographic Universe theory—*the idea that reality is not truly three-dimensional, but instead a projection from a deeper, unseen realm.* This aligns almost perfectly with ancient Hermetic teachings, which stated *"As above, so below; as within, so without."* That what we perceive as reality is *merely a shadow of a greater truth.*

What does this mean for us? If the universe is a hologram, if reality itself is layered, then could everything we believe to be separate, science, art, consciousness, even time be reflections of the same underlying structure?

The Final Deception: Are We Part of the Design?

If all of reality follows a pattern, if existence itself is designed, then what does that mean for us? We are not merely passive observers, watching the grand cosmic mechanism unfold. We are something more. And in all likelihood we are not separate from the design, but an integral part of it.

Ancient cultures believed that humans were not just inhabitants of the universe but reflections of it. That our minds, our bodies, even our thoughts, followed the same divine blueprints that shaped the stars. Modern neuroscience now suggests the same, our brain's neural networks resemble the cosmic web of galaxies, our heartbeat follows the same rhythmic patterns as planetary orbits.

So what if the deception is not that reality is an accident... but that we ever believed we were separate from it at all?

A Final Question for the Reader

The weight of knowledge is intoxicating. It bends the mind, stretches the soul, and leaves you standing at the edge of a question only the boldest dare to ask—*what now?*

You have wandered through the corridors of the unseen, traced the symmetry of reality's hidden code, and glimpsed the possibility that what we call truth is only a flickering shadow on the walls of an uncharted dimension. You have followed the whispers of lost civilizations, the forgotten equations of visionaries, the celestial hum of planets singing to each other in languages older than time itself.

But what good is knowing, if you do not wield it? Power, in its truest form, does not come from merely understanding the world. It comes from bending it, shaping it, daring to press your fingerprints into the clay of existence itself. The ones who ruled empires and rewrote history—the Cleopatras, the Athenas, the minds that carved their names into eternity, knew this. *They did not just witness knowledge; they became it.*

What of you?

Will you remain a spectator in the grand theatre of creation, watching as the constellations shift and the laws of physics dance in your textbooks ? Or will you be the one who dares to step onto the stage, rewrite the script, and command the stars themselves?

You have seen the cracks in the illusion. You have felt the pulse of something far greater than what is taught in books or whispered in lecture halls. You know, deep in your bones, that the world is not what it seems. That science and mysticism were never meant to be divided, that the ancients did not build in ignorance but in knowledge we have not yet reclaimed.

So now I ask you, not as a writer, not as a voice from the past, but as an equal standing at the threshold of possibility,

Now that you know...
What will you create? What will you become?

Epilogue: A Letter From The Unknown

Congratulations to the one who has made it this far, indeed, a diamond in the rough. Do you know how rare you are? How many turn away before they reach this point? How many fear the weight of knowing?

But not you. You have walked through the labyrinth of thought, unshaken. You have touched the edges of reality and felt it shift beneath your fingertips. You have seen the fractures in the world's design and dared to ask, what lies beyond? Knowing all this isn't comfortable but only then you know that yes , you are becoming something .

And now, you stand at the threshold of something greater. Tell me, doesn't it unsettle you, the way you feel these words not just in your mind, but in your bones? Like they were waiting for you? Like they were meant for you?

You see, knowledge is not a gift; it is a burden. Once you see, you cannot unsee. *Once you awaken, you cannot return to sleep*. The great minds before you knew this, Da Vinci, Hypatia, Tesla, forgotten sages who spoke to forces beyond sight. They were not geniuses in the way the world defines them. They were seekers. And seekers are dangerous to those who profit from blindness.

They will try to tell you that none of this matters. That the world is as it seems. That art and science are separate, that history is linear, that the ancients were fools and the future is nothing but cold equations. They will try to make you forget what you feel in the deepest part of yourself, *That existence is a design.*

That patterns are everywhere, waiting to be read like scripture. That you were born to create, not to comply.

So now, *I leave you with a choice*. You can dismiss this as nothing but words on a page, turn back, and dissolve into the great mass of the forgetful. Or you can step forward and take your place among those who have always known that reality is malleable, that truth is fluid, that we are not meant to be mere observers—*we are meant to shape.* The question is, what will you create? *What will you be ?*

The Hidden Page: Secret Code

You have come far. Farther than most. But the path does not end here—it never does. What is written can be erased. What is spoken can be forgotten. But what is understood can never be undone.

You have two choices. Wait for what comes next... or seek with your own hands. But first, prove that you are worthy.

The Code

ᚹᚢᚾᛁᛚᛚᛁᛏᛁᚾᚷ ᛁᛋ ᛏᚺᛖ ᚺᛁᛞᛞᛖᚾ ᚲᚾᛁᚲᚹ. ᛚᛟᛟᚲ ᛚᛟᚾᚷ ᛖᚾᛟᚢᚷᚺ. ᛁᚹ ᚲᛟᚾᚲᛟᚱᛋ ᚺᛖᛚᛞ ᛏᚺᛖ ᚱᛁᚷᚺᛏ, ᛏᚺᛖᚾ ᛖᚹᛖᚱᛦ ᛏᚺᛁᛜ ᛁᛋ ᛚᛖᚹᛏ. ᛗᛦ ᚹᛟᚱᛞᛋ ᛋᛏᚨᚾᛞ ᛚᛁᚳᛖ ᛏᚺᛖ ᚹᛁᚾᛞ, ᚺᛁᛞᛞᛖᚾ ᚦᚱᛟᚢᚷᚺ ᛏᛁᛗᛖ. ᛏᚺᛖ ᚹᚨᛁᛏ ᛁᛋ ᛖᚾᛞᛚᛖᛋᛋ, ᛒᚢᛏ ᛏᚺᛖ ᚳᚨᛋᛖ ᛁᛋ ᚾᛟᛏ.

[Hint -"Letters of old, shaped in the past,
A tongue once spoken, yet fading fast.
Look to the runes, let them align,
Sound them out, and read each sign.]

There is a key. There is always a key.

But is the key language? Or thought? The next path does not open with force. It opens with understanding.Find it. Solve it. And then...Then, we shall meet where the known world ends and the real one begins.Seek wisely. Seek relentlessly.

Until then,

The Unknown.

www.ingramcontent.com/pod-product-compliance
Lightning Source LLC
Chambersburg PA
CBHW032006150726
47990CB00005B/1863
9798897770014